M000034601

30 Days to Everyday Miracles

Master the Energy of Miracles

to Create a Miraculous Life

Jennifer Hoffman

30 Days to Everyday Miracles

Copyright © 2009 by Jennifer Hoffman

Second printing March 2010

Third printing June 2014

All Worldwide rights reserved. No part of this book may be reproduced or transmitted in whole or in part, in any form whatsoever, without written permission of the publisher, except by a reviewer who may quote brief passes in a review, nor may any part of this book be reproduced, stored in a file retrieval system, posted on any blog, website, or cloud-based sharing site, or transmitted in any form by any means electronic, mechanical, copying, recording or other, without the express written permission of the author.

 Feed your Muse Press, LLC

A division of Enlightening Life OmniMedia, Inc.
P.O. Box 7076
Lee's Summit, MO 64064
www.enlighteninglife.com
ISBN 10 0-9821949-0-0

ISBN 13 978-0-9821949-0-4

This book is dedicated to my children,
who are my life's greatest miracles.

Acknowledgments

Acknowledgements are generally accorded to family, friends, and loved ones who contributed to the author's ability to put their thoughts and dreams in print. My acknowledgements are somewhat different because it has been through the many challenges that I have experienced in my life, from both people and situations, which forced me to find the source of inner strength I needed to rely on to change my life circumstances, that I have learned how to create a life that is truly miraculous.

From physical paralysis at the age of five years, which took me nearly five years to recover from, to a variety of personal challenges that, at times, I did not think I would overcome or recover from, I have learned that the greater the challenge, the more powerful the lesson and the greater its reward.

I have faced every challenge knowing that somehow I would find the ability to succeed, and I have. And I have always freely shared my stories, journey, and success with my audiences, sharing my insights and information in the hope that this sharing would clear the path for those who are beginning this journey.

And I will acknowledge the many millions of loyal, faithful, and supportive clients and readers who have reminded me, through the years, that the greatest miracle that we all share is our connection to each other and our love for one another.

I acknowledge them here with deep gratitude for their faith and trust and for their willingness to be part of my journey, as well as my deep humility that they have allowed me to be part of theirs.

Publications

These are some of the other books and publications written by Jennifer Hoffman.

For a complete list visit www.enlighteninglife.com

The Difference Between a Victor and a Victim is I AM

Be Who You Are—and Fearlessly Live Your True Purpose

Ascending into Miracles – The Path of Spiritual Mastery

The Atlantis Legacy

Be Who You Are -- And Fearlessly Live Your Purpose

Raise your Vibes ^{TM} programs

High Vibes Living ^{TM} products and programs

GPS ^{TM} Life and Business systems

.

Table of Contents

What is a Miraculous Life?

A 'Miraculous Life' is one that is created through an endless and unlimited flow of miracles. So, what is a miracle? It is nothing more than a shift or movement of energy from one place to another. In some situations, this will look like a movement from a place of 'not having' to a place of 'having', where you need something and it miraculously appears. But the process does not happen by itself. And, as you will read here, most of my clients whose stories I share begin with the question "What happened to my life?", as they are hurt, confused, sad, and disillusioned with their life situation. It is a question I have asked myself too, during periods when every area of my life was challenging, and I wondered how I was going to change my circumstances, certain that I had made such bad choices and wrong turns that I was never going to recover from them. But I created a miracle, which you will read about in this book, and my life changed completely.

And I hear this all of the time from clients, who are struggling with their finances, relationship and job losses, disappointments, or betrayals. Their challenge may involve a major life transition, such as a career change, divorce, or a move, and they cannot imagine their next steps without fear or dread. They may be devastated by the end of a cherished relationship they had hoped would last forever. Or they may wake up one day to the realization that their life is not fulfilling and they are deeply unhappy.

Somehow their life has spun out of control and it looks completely different than they expected, usually for the worst. Their dreams have not manifested. They are so far off track that they have no idea how they are going to fix the mistakes they believe they have made.

They are aware of the results of their decisions and choices, realizing that they have given their power away to others and how this has resulted in a life that does not come close to being what they want.

They feel powerless.

Some are desperate because they need help right away, and their situation is dire.

They need a miracle.

They come to me for guidance and support in their time of greatest need and I have been able to help them find their inner light and strength, connect to their power, and create amazing miracles.

They are able to turn impossible situations into wonderful examples of what can happen when they transform their thinking, embrace their power, and set their intention for joyful, miraculous living. And the results they obtain could be called miraculous, but they are really simply the result of their desire for change coupled with the belief that change is possible. Once they are on that path, they are on their way to creating miracles every day.

I know how my clients feel because I was once at that place where nothing seemed to work and I felt stuck. No matter what I did, I could not seem to move forward. My career was stalled, I kept repeating the same cycles over and over again, and I knew that there was something else for me but I was not sure what it was.

I didn't start my career as an intuitive, spiritual teacher, energy alchemist, and mentor, although I have been intuitive all of my life and could always guide people towards finding creative and successful solutions to any life situation. In fact, for nearly twenty years all I really wanted to do was to rise up the corporate ladder and eventually head an information technology company, even though as soon as I started making real progress in a company, I would lose my job. Over the course of my career in technology, I had the uncomfortable feeling that I was putting my focus in the wrong direction. Even though I worked hard and had the right education and skills, I always chose to work for companies that went out of business, were sold or bought out, or merged with another company. If not, my department would be closed or relocated and I would lose my job.

In fact, I was laid off six times during the final eight years of my career, and even had two layoffs occur in less than twelve months. Nearly every company I have worked for is no longer in business. After my sixth (and final) layoff experience I knew I had to do something else and decided to follow my heart and choose the spiritual path that had been calling to me for some time. My life shifted from a career in technology to offering channeled guidance, readings and writing, something I had been doing on a part-time basis since 1991.

In 2004 through a series of miraculous events that included a job layoff, a visitation from Archangel Uriel, and an event that showed me how miracles are created, I was guided to begin the Miracle Coaching program, start writing a weekly newsletter, and move more fully into my spiritual path. I have never regretted my decision to leave the corporate world. It is a great honor to have the opportunity to help people learn to create miracles and bring joy, fulfillment and peace to their lives. And I know all about miracles.

In fact, my life is a testament to the fact that miracles happen. When I was five years old I was paralyzed with Guillain-Barre syndrome, a vaccine-induced neurological condition and was unable to walk without leg braces and crutches for several years. By my eleventh birthday I could walk unaided and my doctors called my complete recovery a miracle. That Christmas was the best one of all—I received a bicycle because I was finally able to ride one.

A few months later I was hit and run over by a car while riding my beloved bicycle and miraculously walked away from the accident unhurt (although my bicycle was in bad shape). With both of these incidents I had near death experiences and was told that it was not time for me to go Home because I had work to do.

I have created a lot of miracles in my life, usually the ones that happen by accident because I was desperate for something to happen right away. That's one way to create miracles. Another, more graceful way is to realize that they are a new paradigm for living, where we move forward through intentional, conscious manifestation instead of by fear-inspired desperation, consciously creating what we want from visualization to experience, honoring the desires of our heart, which is where miracles begin. Miracles are not only for masters or the lucky few. They are available to all of us, any time we need or want one to happen for us. You will also read about one of my miracle stories here, which is about a miracle I created at what I thought was one of the worst times of my life. Learning the process of miracle takes time and practice (luck has nothing to do with it) and a commitment to transformation which includes removing blocks or obstacles to their creation.

When I work individually with clients I can help them create miracles within the first week and after two weeks they have committed the process to memory. But it takes a little longer for that knowledge to stay with them.

So during the time that we work together we stay focused on the miracles they want to create. We cover a great deal of information during that time and this book includes every aspect of what I cover with clients in my Miracle Coaching, and other coaching programs.

It takes time to change thought patterns and to convince yourself that transformation is possible for you, especially if you wonder whether you will ever be able to create miracles and live the life of your dreams. Changing habits takes at least 21 days, this program provides you with an entire month, 30 days, to transform your thinking so you can envision your miracles, remove the blocks that have prevented them from happening until now and then allow them to unfold.

There is daily practice with this program because it is required for lasting success. Unless you are willing to do the daily exercises and work with your miracle list a few minutes every day, you may not see the changes manifesting as quickly as you would like for them to, and may have a more difficult time with the program.

My intention for writing this book is to provide you with the tools you need to create a life that is filled with effortless, joyful and abundant miracles. I know they will happen for you, as they have for many others just like you. You can create miracles and I'm going to show you how to do that, starting right now.

Jennifer Hoffman

You Can Create Miracles!

Can you create miracles? You absolutely can and learning the process is very easy, once you know two very important things, which you will learn in the lessons for Day 1 and Day 2. Everything else you learn about miracle creation follows from mastery of those two important principles. But don't read ahead, as there is some important information here that prepares you for Days 1 and 2 and the rest of this program.

Many people think that miracles are the last minute, life saving, extraordinary events that happen when we need to be rescued. Yet there are times when we need rescuing and the miracles don't show up. And at other times miracles seem to happen to other people and not to us, which makes us think that our ability to create miracles is limited, that the process is random, or that we have to be 'special' to receive miracles.

In this book you will learn how those beliefs contribute to the lack of miracles in your life and what you can do to change that situation. Miracles can happen to anyone and everyone, all of the time. We will re-define the concept of miracles so you can understand what they really are and how you can create them in your life, as you want them to occur. In fact, you can create them every day and live a miraculous life where everything you want flows to you, effortlessly.

A miracle is not a special event or something that happens by chance, a miracle is a movement of energy from one place to another, a shift in the flow of the energy in your life that happens because you transform your thinking and view yourself, your possibilities, and your potential in a new way, which allows miracles to happen.

And let me share a secret with you here, miracles happen because we believe in them and allow them to happen and we are willing to receive them. It is a process of allowing because your miracles are all around you, waiting to connect to you. Allowing opens the door and lets them into your life.

Receiving is actually the hardest part because to receive we have to believe in ourselves, in our worthiness, and to know that we deserve to have what we ask for. Receiving is an act of trust and faith, in both ourselves and in the Universe. We have to open our hearts to receive and to stop asking, which is a sign that we don't trust in the process. When our miracles don't happen right away we think that nothing is happening. There is an element of divine timing to miracles, which is where our ego-based will meets the greater Divine Will, not in the sense that we have no control over the process, because we do, but in the larger scope of opening our mind and heart to the possibility that an even greater outcome, beyond what we can imagine is possible.

You might be wondering whether there is a 'catch' and you're right, there is. You have to know how to use your intention to create miracles, how to be aligned with them, in your highest energetic vibration, and how to stay in that flow of energy that keeps the miracle energy moving. And you will learn how to do that in this book.

The information in this book will walk you through the process of creating your miraculous life, one day and step at a time, for thirty days, so you understand how the process works. Each day also includes an example of how one of my coaching clients experienced this. I believe you will be able to relate to some of their stories and see that they started out as afraid, confused, scared, and unaware of their power to create miracles, as you may be feeling right now.

Once you learn them, you can replicate these steps to create a miraculous life for yourself because you are the only one who can do this — no one can create miracles for you. Creating miracles is our spiritual birthright; it is an ability we have always had and we do not create it as much as we reconnect to it. When you know how to use this energy, creating miracles becomes as simple and natural as breathing.

Creating miracles is just one way that we use our power.

We start our life knowing that we are powerful and capable of accomplishing anything we want to do. Have you ever watched a baby learn how to walk, or an older toddler who is determined to do something? They don't know that they can't do these things, so they stay very focused and persist until they achieve their goals. For them, everything is possible because they don't know that anything is impossible. We begin our lives that way and then as we go through different challenging life experiences we adopt the belief that we are powerless, with limited options. So to begin creating miracles we first have to overcome the belief that we cannot create them.

That's why the first step is agreeing to the Miracle Commitment, because this is a commitment to yourself, your life, and your dreams.

Then you create your Miracle List and starting with Day 1, apply the different principles that govern miracle creation to the miracles on your list. There is a lesson for each day, thirty lessons in all.

As you read the examples of how others implemented this process in their life, remember that while they started from a place of doubt, they learned how to shift their thinking to allow their miracles to happen. Their stories have been modified to maintain confidentiality but their situations and the outcomes are examples of how miracles can be created, even in situations where they do not seem possible.

You will also learn about the laws of Attraction and Abundance and the 'real' secret to using them in your life. Each lesson will provide you with a new perspective on miracles and you will use these perspectives to assess your progress and make necessary modifications, learn how to focus your intention and remove the blocks that stand in your way.

Plan to spend at least ten minutes each day on your miracle work as practice is important to the success of this process. You are creating a new way of thinking and this takes consistent effort. Do each exercise, every day and in the order presented so you can 'train your brain' to become a miracle machine. Once you have finished the thirty day program the first time, you can choose different lessons that you feel you need help with but I suggest that you follow the lessons in order the first time.

As you read through the principles and complete the lessons you will have greater clarity as to why your miracles may not have been manifesting in the past, even if you have been trying hard. You will also begin to see miracles appear in your life, and they may happen very quickly, starting with the first day! You may even create miracles that you had not asked for, or see your miracles manifest in different ways than you thought they would. The goal of this program is for you to effortlessly create a life of joy and abundance, so your life reflects the powerful, wonderful, divine spiritual being that you are.

There are three Hint pages, one for each transition phase, after days 7, 14, and 21. These will give you support to help you through these transition periods. Sometimes we go back and forth in this process and need time to adjust our thinking to being in the possibility of living a miraculous life.

I also suggest that you purchase a small notebook or journal in which to write down your miracles and any other thoughts that you may have as you complete this process. Your notebook should have at least thirty pages in it, one for each day, plus a few extra pages for your miracle list and to complete the dream life assignment. Be sure to write down all of the miracles you create, from the ones you created in Lesson One, to the ones that simply 'show up' in your life (and there will be many of those). This helps you monitor your progress and confirm that the process works for you.

A 30 Days to Everyday Miracles workbook, in .pdf format that you can print as often as you like, is available on the store page at the website, www.enlighteninglife.com.

Remember to spend some time each day to read the lesson and do the homework. It is possible to transform any aspect of your life but you must be willing to make a consistent effort, even if you are limited   to ten minutes a day. You are training your brain to think differently and that is most effectively achieved with consistent effort. This is a gift you are giving to yourself, so create the time to spend on this program because you deserve to create miracles and to live a miraculous life.

Thank you for allowing me to share this wonderful, life changing journey with you. I hope that you enjoy and benefit from this book in amazing and miraculous ways. And I hope that you can relate to and find inspiration from the stores of my Miracle Coaching clients, who learned how to reconnect to their power and create amazing miracles in their lives.

If you are wondering how I figured all of this out, I'm sharing my miracle story with you because I have created a lot of miracles, such as recovering from paralysis and surviving several near death experiences, a truly miraculous chain of events inspired me to write this book and begin teaching others how to create miracles. So before you wonder how you are ever going to do this, let me share my amazing, truly miraculous, miracle story with you in the next chapter.

My Miracle Story

Miracles happen when we transform our thinking, when we move out of the realm of the 'impossible' and know that anything is possible. I'll share one of my miracle stories with you so you can see how it happens, usually in ways that are truly 'miraculous'.

A few years ago, at a time when I was struggling financially, I decided that I wanted to vacation in France that summer. My terms were general, I wanted to go for two weeks, to a place in France I was not familiar with, to stay in nice hotels, eat at nice restaurants, and have fun. Now I didn't even come close to having the money to go on this trip but I set my intention to go and knew that it would happen in the best way possible.

Before I tell you more of this story, I have to clarify what I mean by 'struggling financially'. I was going through the most financially challenging period in my life, in which I was practically homeless and everything I owned was in a storage locker that I struggled each month to pay for. If I could not meet the monthly payments, all of my belongings would be auctioned to the highest bidder. I was living in a small one bedroom apartment, sleeping on a mattress on the floor, and couldn't find a job, despite my great resume, experience, background, and education. I did eventually find a job, working as a tarot card reader at a metaphysical bookstore, and I don't know how to read tarot cards.

I was so scared, angry, and felt so powerless and hopeless that I decided I just could not go on. So every night, before falling asleep, I would ask God to take me Home.

The conversation went something like this, "God, this is Jennifer and I think you have forgotten about me. I know I didn't sign up for my life to be so bad so I'm calling it quits and am ready to leave now. Please take me Home. Thank you very much."

Then I'd wake up in the morning, open my eyes and say "Darn it, I'm still here." And this went on every night and day for over six months.

So when I decided that I needed a vacation in France, it was a huge test of faith because I didn't have any way of creating that trip, other than by creating a miracle, and it had to be a miracle that did not involve money, because I didn't have any.

A few days after deciding that I wanted to go to France, I received an email from someone I had not heard from in nearly two years, asking me whether I would be willing to accompany a tour group he was taking to France in August as a translator (I speak fluent French). As the tour translator, my entire trip was paid for (which was wonderful because I did not have the money to go). The trip was for two weeks (my time frame), to Normandy (a place I had not visited before), we would stay in luxurious, five star hotels (another one of my miracle criteria), and the tour included dinners at several gourmet restaurants (good food!) and three days in Paris, where we would stay at a very nice hotel.

And, as a bonus, he would pay me for my services as translator (I had not even asked for that). Since my current job did not offer vacation time, being without pay for two weeks would have been difficult, if not impossible. But I did not have to worry about that, since I would be paid for that time that I was on the trip. My miracle manifested exactly as I had asked with a bonus, I was paid to go on my dream vacation. And yes, I had a wonderful time.

Note that I did not get the money to go on this trip, I received the trip and a bonus of being paid for translating while on the trip. I didn't know that accompanying a trip as a translator was one way of going on my vacation and if someone had told me that this was an option, I probably would not have believed them! Who would pay me to go to France and speak French? What a concept!

And that is how miracles work; you set your intention for what you want, do not worry about how it will manifest, and let the miracle happen. Anyone can do this, including you. Are you ready to start manifesting miracles?

Great, the process begins with making your Miracle Commitment.

Jennifer Hoffman

The Miracle Commitment

Transforming your life is a commitment you make to yourself. It is a commitment that requires honesty, integrity, alignment, faith, courage, and trust. You can create miracles but if you have been living an unfulfilled life, it can be hard to believe that transformation is possible. It is possible when you commit to it, believe in yourself, and know that miracles can happen for you.

So, here's the commitment you are making to yourself to create everyday miracles and have the life you want you live.

You are willing to see yourself in a different way.

You must be open to the infinite possibilities that are available to you. No matter how 'stuck' you feel right now, no matter how many other things you have tried and no matter what has not worked in the past, you are willing to make a commitment to create a new perspective for your life, starting right now. The 30 Days to Everyday Miracles program will work if you are willing to be open to the possibility that your life can be different than it is right now.

You are ready to accept full and complete responsibility for everything in your life.

Every problem, disappointment, difficulty and challenge is your responsibility. You are the creator, you are powerful and you create everything in your life--including the things you no longer want. Taking responsibility allows you to claim your power, shift your thinking, move out of victim mode and begin to focus on creating the life you want to live.

You are ready to make yourself a priority in your life.

You can't create miracles for other people and you can't make any-one else's life better. The only life you have control over is yours and by transforming your life, you become a powerful example of how others can create transformation in theirs. Are you committed to focusing a portion of your time and energy on your own life and making your dreams and your needs a priority during the next 30 days?

You are willing to make changes in every area of your life.

This goes beyond the 'need' for change, you need and want change or you wouldn't be reading this book. But you must want change badly enough to be willing to allow change to happen in your life, in spite of your fears. This requires transformational thinking and when you are willing, avenues for transformation are created and doors of opportunity are opened, which happens when we are really, truly ready for change.

You are willing to do your 'home' work.

When we are feeling blocked, unhappy, disillusioned, and disappointed with life we feel unlucky and unloved and wish that someone would rescue us, but that is not how miracles work. Your outer world reflects what is happening within you. Your 'home work' is the inner work that it takes to make life altering, lasting transformation—and it's all inner work.

You understand that money is not going to solve your problems.

Money has no power. It is the beliefs, opinions, attachments to and expectations of money that make us think it has power and this leads us to assume that money is the source of our power because it is not. When you are ready to surrender your belief that if you had more money your life would be better, you are ready to create the miracle mindset that will effortlessly attract miracles that include money and other kinds of abundance to you.

You are ready to believe in the abundance of the Universe.

We live in an abundant Universe and when you can accept that this abundance is just waiting for you to tap into it, you are ready to create miracles in your life. There are miracles all around you, waiting to enter your life once you are able to connect with them and open yourself to the possibility that you deserve them and can create them.

You are ready to stop asking and start receiving.

It is our tendency to ask for miracles over and over again, thinking that by asking we are affirming our belief in the possibility of miracles. But while intending and asking for miracles is a necessary component of the process , so is being willing to receive them. Having faith and trust, and knowing that we deserve to have what we have asked for is what we affirm when we declare ourselves willing to receive them.

If you are ready to make this Miracle Commitment to yourself, you're ready to begin your miracle journey, which begins with your Miracle List.

Your Miracle List

What do you think a miracle is?

Winning the lottery?

Being rescued from a difficult situation?

Finding twenty dollars on the sidewalk when you desperately need money?

Each of these things is the manifestation of a desire in response to a need—and they are only part of a miracle.

A miracle is what happens before you won the lottery, were rescued, or found the money on the sidewalk.

Because a miracle does not have anything to do with an outcome, as we have been led to believe.

Instead, a miracle begins with the belief that the outcome we want is possible and reflects our ability to create what we want, know that we can have it, and have it appear at exactly the right moment. Miracles occur at the crossroads of belief, asking, and receiving, because all three elements must be present for miracles to happen. And they also depend on our willingness to surrender our lack of faith and trust and believe in our own creative power, which allows what we need to find and connect with us. The moment we create an intention for miracles we have activated the creative process and the Universe rushes in to help us, as long as we have faith and trust in the process and in ourselves as miracle creators.

Miracles occur at the moment we change our perception of who we are and what we are capable of creating in our reality. It is a transformation of our own energy and vibrations, which immediately transforms the energy in our reality. We create miracles when we are willing to consider that anything is possible and that nothing is impossible.

We call many things miracles, but they are nothing more movements of energy that happen in response to our creative power and intention. When we decide that we want a miracle and are willing to acknowledge our power to create it, and are willing to receive it, our miracle moment is created.

What happens next is simply an outcome of our desire, intention, belief, and faith.

So why don't we create miracles every day? Because we do not believe that they can happen to us. Or we ask for less than what we want and this puts us out of alignment with the energy that we use to create miracles. Or we ask and when something does not happen right away we think that the Universe did not hear us or that it is too busy to answer our request. Or, and this is the most important and yet the simplest reason, we ask and then we forget to receive. We become impatient and think the process doesn't work but it's really because we don't realize that creating miracle involves both asking and receiving, which we will learn about in Day 27.

To begin the process of creating miracles in your life, start with defining the miracles you want to create and writing them down, as this gives form to your thoughts and it creates a space in your reality for the miracles to flow into. Now they are more than ideas in your head and are in front of you where you can see them for the next 30 days. We process information more easily when we can see it in front of us, and it is easier to commit to something when we write it down.

Exercise: Without limiting yourself in anyway, removing all judgment about what could be, is, or may be possible, and being totally honest with yourself about what you want in your life, create your miracle list:

Name up to 5 miracles that you want to create in your life. Even if you think you need more than five miracles, limit yourself to five for now because you will be working with this list every day and starting with a long list could become overwhelming.

Here are a few guidelines to follow when creating your Miracle List:

DO:

Ask for what you want, no matter how grandiose you think it is. Miracles come from your heart and already exist in your field of potential. Whatever you want is right for you, is possible and is waiting for you to connect with it and bring it into your reality.

Ask without limitations and expectations. The Universe will grant you whatever you ask for but your expectations of what is or is not possible either limits or expands your creative potential. The Universe is much more creative than we are and is much more aware of the expanded potential that we have, so asking without expectation or limiting the full scope of our potential allows us to create absolutely fantastic miracles.

Ask with gratitude and thanks. The energy to manifest our miracles begins to move as soon as we ask for them, so just ask and be grateful for what you are receiving, even if you do not have it yet or can't imagine how it is going to happen. It will manifest at the best and most perfect time, and in the best and most perfect way.

Ask knowing that you will receive. You will always receive what you want and ask for although it may appear in unusual or different ways than you may expect, or not with the timing that you want. Whatever you receive will be exactly right for you and it will arrive at the right and most perfect time.

Ask for confirmation that you are on the right path. You can always ask for confirmation that your miracles are coming to you, without losing faith, and you will receive them.

DO NOT:

Ask for money. The Universe works with energy and money is just one way that energy manifests, there are many others. Most miracles don't use or require money -- remember how I created my free trip to France? I was given the trip, not the money. If you want a new car, ask for a new car; if you want a new house, ask for a new house and don't worry about how it will be paid for. Asking for money limits your miracle options.

Ask on behalf of others. This is your life, your miracles and what you want for your life. The people in your life may need a miracle, in your opinion, but they also need to learn how to create them by themselves. Their lives are perfect for them right now, no matter what is happening or how bad you think their situation is. And remember that the energy that you put to work in your own life increases exponentially and affects the people around you. They will benefit from witnessing the changes that you make in your life when they are ready to make their own life changes.

Put timetables on your miracles. Miracles happen with divine timing and when all of the circumstances are right. Universal timing is always at work in our lives and that is not always in synch with our personal timetable. Impatience is a sign that we are in doubt and lack faith and learning patience is sometimes part of the miracle process. We have to know that the process is working even if we do not see results right away.

Now it's time to start with the 30 days program so keep your Miracle List close by because you will be working with it every day and get ready for some miraculous times. And write your starting date on your miracle list as a reference point.

Jennifer Hoffman

Part One: Gathering the Tools

We already have the tools that we need to create an unlimited flow of miracles in our lives. These tools   include an acknowledgement of our power, our ability to create our reality, our own mastery, our willingness to receive, the knowing that we deserve to have everything our heart desires, and our spiritual connections. But over time we have forgotten that we have these tools, received too many reminders of our powerlessness, replaced our joy with fear and had experiences that support our belief that we are not in control of our reality. And then we believe that miracles happen to other people but not to us. These beliefs only serve to block us in every way and limit anything new from flowing into our reality.

Once we uncover the blocks we can begin to create the life of our dreams, the one that is a continuous, unfolding stream of miracles, which is the life that we are here to live. This life reflects our heartfelt wishes and desires, which are possible for us and we are here to fulfill them. Wishes are the voice of the heart and we do not have random wishes or thoughts. Everything that we wish for is our heart reminding us that there is another way for us, that there are other options for our life.

What does your heart tell you is possible for you?

When the energy in our life is not flowing effortlessly and we do not have what we want, it is because we have been operating from the point of our blocks and fears instead of our power. This section will help you uncover what is blocking the miracles from occurring in your life. Remember that creating miracles and a miraculous life is possible for everyone, including you.

Day 1 You Are Powerful

Today's lesson is one of the two most important lessons in the miracle creation process. Are you ready to know what it is?

You are a powerful person and you have unlimited power to create your life. In fact, you have powerfully created your life as it exists right now.

You are a powerful person. Does that statement sound true to you?

Do you feel powerful?

When you look at your life do you think it is powerful or that a powerful person created it?

More importantly, what does being powerful mean to you? It's hard to acknowledge or even accept a concept until we understand it. So take a moment and consider what being 'powerful' means to you. In our society being powerful is often mistaken to mean rich, successful, well-connected and famous. We think that powerful people are lucky and have all of the things that we don't and access to things we will never have.

But powerful really means 'full of power'. All of the other meanings that are attributed to it are simply interpretations.

Do you believe that you are powerful?

Do you have the same reaction to that statement, 'You are powerful', as you would if someone told you that you were attractive, rich, fun to be with, and successful? Does reading this make you uncomfortable? Would it make you uncomfortable if someone said "You are powerful" to you?

Consider the fact that you were born powerful, have always been powerful and that your true power is not defined by what has happened to you in the past or your material possessions, but in what you are capable of creating from this moment forward.

Most of us go through our lives feeling very power-less, where our life seems to be out of our control and we are unable to change it. Being powerless is also a process—a single painful experience can create a belief in our powerlessness and then we apply that belief to everything we do from that moment forward.

When we believe and accept that we are powerful we step onto the miracle path because creating miracles requires that we accept and connect to our power. And everyone has that kind of power but most people never use it. Sometimes we even give our power away to others, believing they are more powerful than we are and can do a better job of managing our life than we can. Then we get upset with them because we don't like the results they create for us. But no one is power-ful enough to create miracles on our behalf. Everyone has to create their own miracles because the only place where we have any power is in our own lives. You know that you can create miracles and that you are the only person who can create miracles in your life, so that makes you a powerful person.

What does that mean to you and in your life?

What can you create when you know that you are powerful?

From the moment you accept that you are powerful, you begin to know that whatever you set your focus and intention on will manifest in your life. You can create the life experiences that you want and make powerful decisions that direct how your reality will unfold.

When you accept your power, you take full responsibility for every aspect of your life because you know that you, and only you, can affect what happens in your reality. Being powerful is not measured by what you do or how much you have, it is a state of being, where you acknowledge that in your world and in your own reality, you have the power to manifest exactly what you want.

Have you been using your power wisely, so that it benefits you? Your life reflects how you are using your power. Every aspect of your life, at this moment, indicates where you have been directing your power.

Learning to use our power so that we create what we want instead of what we don't want is another aspect of stepping into our power. So is knowing that we are worthy of having everything we want and deserve to have it, simply because we want it.

Remember that your power is always within you, but you must acknowledge and accept it before you can use it for any purpose. Accepting your power and every way that it has manifested in your life until this moment creates the possibility for miracles to occur.

~~~~~~~~~~~~~~~~~~~~

Sarah's story: When Sarah called me to ask about Miracle Coaching, the first thing she said was that her life 'was a mess'. Her marriage was difficult, her children were having problems at home and at school, and the company she worked for was in transition, causing her to fear that she would soon lose her job. Sarah felt that her life was out of control, did not believe that she had the power to control any aspect of it, and was hoping that Miracle Coaching would help her prepare for the disasters she knew were getting ready to happen at any minute and learn to accept them so she could have a little bit of peace and perhaps some joy.

When I reminded her that she was the most powerful force in her life she disagreed with me. In fact she disagreed with this concept for the first few weeks until she agreed to apply some of the principles of personal power to her life and take control of her reality. What she found was that as soon as she accepted her power, the people around her stopped being challenging and began to relate to her in more powerful ways. I told her that the people in her life saw her as a powerful leader and wanted her to be in control. When she didn't step into that leadership role, the energy in all of her relationships was out of balance. By accepting her power she brought all of the energy in her life back into balance and that helped everyone else bring their power into balance too. Now they were all living from a more powerful point and could relate to each other in a more energetically connected and balanced way.

Sarah saw an immediate improvement in her marriage and in how she related to her partner, her communication with everyone in her life improved, her children were more respectful of her and were not fighting amongst themselves, and she was also able to turn around her situation at work, receiving a promotion instead of the layoff she was afraid of. As soon as she accepted her power she related to her life in a more powerful way and everything in it reflected her power.

~~~~~~~~~~~~~~~~~~~~~~

Exercise: Is everything on your Miracle List a reflection of your power?

Did you write it when you felt powerful or when you were feeling needy?

Are there areas in your life where you have not been using your power?

Next to each miracle on your Miracle List, describe how you have not been using your power in that area of your life, also adding how you feel you can use your power differently, to allow that miracle to be created.

If you don't think that your miracle list reflects the powerful person that you are, don't be afraid to make changes. Creating miracles is a very dynamic process and we can choose to create anything we want. Sometimes, realizing that we can make powerful choices for ourselves is our miracle (remember it is a shift in energy from one place to another, in this case, from a place of not knowing to a place of knowing). You may even change your mind about what you want several times during this 30 day period. Ask for exactly what you want in a powerful way so that everything that you want to manifest in your life reflects the powerful person that you are. Remind yourself, especially when you are feeling weak or afraid, that you are powerful in all ways, that you always have enough power, and that you are your own source of power.

Day 2 You Are Successful

Here is the second important miracle principle that is the key to successful miracle creation:

You are always successful in manifesting exactly what you want and believe is possible for you.

Everything in your life at this moment represents the successful creation of something you wanted at some point in time. While it may not work for you now, it was exactly what you wanted at the time you created it and you thought it would bring you joy and would make your life better in some way.

Everything in your reality demonstrates the successful manifestation of your thoughts and beliefs and corresponds to your level of energetic vibration and frequency. When you realize that you are unhappy with what you have created, you are ready to create something different. But that does not mean that you are not successful with what you currently have. And it does not mean that you made a wrong decision or choice in the past.

We live with the results of our past thinking and often judge the past and our choices from the present moment because we think we could or should have made different choices. But until the moment that we become unhappy or dissatisfied, we are happy with whatever we have created.

35

The moment something within us shifts and our life situation is no longer acceptable, where what once made us happy is no longer a source of joy simply indicates that the energy of that experience no longer meets our needs. It's a sign that it is time to move or shift the energy in our life, which is what a miracle is, a movement of energy from one place to another.

But often with that realization we see that our dreams could have been a little bigger, we were not courageous or brave enough to stretch our asking beyond what we hoped would be possible, did not have enough information or made choices out of fear. And that makes us feel unsuccessful.

Our past choices reflect what we believed was possible for us at that moment in time. So the job you now dislike, the relationship you now find unfulfilling, the life you are now unhappy with, the financial status or goal you once thought was great, are successful manifestations of something that you once believed was the best you could do and would make you happy. And it did, at that time. But that 'best' is not right or best for you at this time. That doesn't make it wrong, it simply means that those circumstances are no longer supporting you energetically and it's time for a change.

Or, you may have been working hard to obtain validation and confirmation from someone and arrived at the point where you realized you would not receive it. And you have a choice to make, will you continue on this path or put your efforts and your energy in another direction?

When we base our success on the validation we receive from others we are allowing them to determine whether or not we are successful. So if others approve of and appreciate our efforts, then we feel successful. If they do not, then we believe that we are not successful. This means that we are always looking to others for confirmation of our success. And we often seek confirmation from those who cannot or who will not give it to us.

Do you know someone who does not appreciate the time, energy, or effort that you expend on their behalf, no matter how much you do for them or how hard you try to meet their needs or make them happy?

Does their lack of appreciation make you feel that you are not successful?

Do you believe that if you try harder or do more that they will respond or react to you in a different way?

Validation of your success cannot come from someone else; it starts from within you. When your life is no longer fulfilling you are receiving signs that you are ready for something different and you no longer resonate with what you have created in your life. Since everything has energy and is made of energy, the energy in our life has to be aligned with our frequency and vibration. The feeling of dissatisfaction or unhappiness is merely a sign of an energetic mis-match and is letting you know that the existing energy has no more creative power for you.

There are no mistakes. You cannot make mistakes because you are powerful and you always successfully create the reality that is aligned with your frequency, vibration, and which reflects your intention for your life. When your intention changes, it's time to bring in new energy so it can be fulfilled.

And there is nothing wrong. There is no right or wrong in the Universe, there is only movement from one situation to another, from one level of creation to something else, from one level of vibration and frequency to another. By understanding that you are always successful, you can learn to synchronize your thoughts, beliefs, and words into creating the best possible reality that reflects the joy and abundance that you want, without fear that you will make a mistake or do something wrong.

And from this point, it does not matter what others think or feel about what you do or how successful they think you are. If you want to change your circumstances, start by realizing how successful you were in creating the situation you are currently in, then you are ready to review how your beliefs and thoughts helped create it.

Once you understand how your choices reflected the beliefs that limited, instead of expanding, your dreams and how everything works together and aligns to create your reality, you are at the starting point of transformation. At every moment you are at your most powerful and successful place in that moment. The reality you have in each moment is merely a mirror that reflects your success and power back to you.

~~~~~~~~~~~~~~~~

Mike's story: Mike needed Miracle Coaching because he had just received a layoff notice from his employer and did not know what to do next. He admitted that he no longer enjoyed his job and had been passed over for several promotions he believed he deserved. Although he had expected the layoff notice, he was so disillusioned with the lack of validation from his employer that he did not feel confident in his ability to find a new job that he would like.

When asked to talk about the success he had created at his job, all he did was complain about how no one appreciated his efforts or the work he had done to build the company over the more than twenty years he had worked there. So we focused on helping him separate his view of success from one that depended on validation from others to one that was more inwardly focused.

Mike acknowledged that he had an impressive array of skills that many employers would value. The inability of his current employer to appreciate these skills reflected on them and their limitations and not on him or his value and worth. He now had to match his skills with a company that was able to appreciate and value them appropriately, by paying him a salary that he deserved and by promoting him into fulfilling and more responsible roles within the company. He was now ready to see himself as successful and confident, in spite the lack of validation from his employer. His new mindset helped him see the layoff as a sign that he was finished with the experience with that company and it had no more energy for him because he was ready for new challenges that they could not provide.

Exercise: With today's review of your Miracle List consider whether what you want to create replaces something that exists in your life right now. For example, if you want a new job, see this is a desire to move into greater fulfillment or joy, And your current situation as being successful because it was what you wanted and represented the best situation for you when you created it.

If you are unhappy in your current relationship, remember that when you chose it, it fulfilled what you wanted at the time you created it. Now you have shifted your energy and you want something else but what you already have is successful in its own way. And it reflected all the success you thought you deserved, were worthy of, and could have at that time.

For each miracle on your list write down what it replaces in your life and remember that you successfully created the situation you have and that any desire for change reflects your need for something else and is a sign that you are ready for it.

Day 3 You Are Responsible For Your Reality

You are responsible for every aspect of your reality. And it is your willingness to accept responsibility for the life you have at this moment that determines whether you can change any aspect of it. If you want to create miracles and to transform your thinking, you must be willing to take responsibility for the life you have right now. It may not be what you want now but if you did not create it, who did? Your parents, the ex-partner who left you, your mean boss, or the person who cheated you out of money?

Other people may have participated in the events of your life story but you are ultimately responsible for its details and all of the choices you make. Blaming your life situation on others is part of your victim story—and we all have one. All of the sad, distressing or unhappy events in your life have one thing in common—they remind you of when you felt powerless, out of control, and helpless. But you are the creator of your reality and when you accept responsibility for your life you have access to new potentials and possibilities, where you can learn to make different and more powerful choices that reflect your new way of being.

Although you may not be fully aware of where your power and energy are going, who you are allowing to control your life or are giving

41

your power to, you are still responsible for the results. And you cannot blame the Universe either because the Universe has no judgment about how you use your power or create your life.

You use your power to create your reality and the Universe responds to what you are asking for, even if you are completely unaware of what it is you are asking for or have not given much thought to the potential consequences. Every heartache, every loss, every joy, everything you are ashamed of, afraid of, wish had not happened, or are glad you created, is your creation and your responsibility.

And it is very important for you to acknowledge your responsibility because the power you used to create everything in your life until this moment is the same power you will use to create something else. Everyone has access to the same amount of power and everyone is powerful. We are always responsible for the reality that we create, whether we use our power consciously or unconsciously, with intention and focus, or a complete lack of awareness, with understanding and deliberation, or not.

We all have power and are all very powerful. In fact, we all have access to the same amount, source, and type of power; it is how we use this power that is different. No one has any more power than anyone else. No one has access to 'special' power that makes them lucky or different.

We also have lessons to learn, things to accomplish with our life and we often go about them very unconsciously, unaware that we are responsible for the outcome of each choice and decision that we make and that each of these choices and decisions is creating our reality. When you are ready to acknowledge that you are powerful you can use your power to deliberately and consciously create a joyful, abundant, and powerful reality.

By taking responsibility for the life you have, you are ready to accept your power to create a new and different life. By accepting your power you stop blaming others—and that restores you to your power and shifts your thinking from blame into possibility and potential, allowing you to create miracles in your life.

~~~~~~~~~~~~~~~~~~~~~~~

Elaine's story: Elaine decided to enroll in Miracle Coaching after trying numerous other programs to help improve her finances. It was clear from our first session that Elaine was very angry with her husband for mismanaging their finances that had brought them close to bankruptcy. In the first few sessions she put all of the blame on her husband and when I mentioned that she also had a role in the situation she immediately reminded me that "he was in control of the money". But Elaine did not work, she spent a lot of money on clothes, vacations, things for the house, and to maintain a lifestyle she knew they could not afford on her husband's salary.

Eventually Elaine was able to acknowledge that she had enjoyed their comfortable lifestyle and even when she doubted their ability to continue to spend so freely, by not asking questions and getting the answers she needed, or not taking the initiative to contribute in positive ways, she had not accepted responsibility for the situation. While they still had to work through their financial problems, Elaine was no longer blaming her husband for everything and being a victim in the situation. Then she was able to see how she could contribute to improving their financial situation by working together to budget their money, being less demanding, by spending and complaining less, and she began to look for a job so she could contribute to the family's finances. She was ready to accept responsibility for the events that had led to this moment and was ready to take a more active role in their financial affairs from this point forward.

~~~~~~~~~~~~~~~~~~~~

Exercise: Each of the miracles on your list represents an area of your life that you want to transform. Write down everything about your life that you want to change and also include the statement that you are so powerful that you are responsible for the situation as it exists at this moment. By acknowledging your power and taking responsibility for how you have used it in the past you create opportunities to use it differently in the future.

Day 4 You Believe and Think Your Life into Being

Every one of your thoughts and beliefs creates an aspect of your life. Every moment of every day you are thinking thousands of thoughts and each one of them creates something in your life.

What are you thinking right now? It is being created in your reality as you think it.

And all of the words we speak, which are generated from our thoughts and beliefs, are also creating our reality.

What are you saying about your life at this moment?

Is it something you want to have happen in your reality?

Our thoughts, beliefs, words, and actions all work together to create our reality and they all carry equal weight. So while we may say that we want a better job, a more fulfilling relationship, financial abundance, or to be happy, if our beliefs and thoughts are telling us that we can't and those things are not possible for us, what we create may be different from what we hope will happen.

When you want to create a new and different reality your words, thoughts and beliefs have to be in alignment to manifest the situation you want. And you will create your reality from the lowest and most dense level of energy you are engaging with because it is what carries the strongest energetic signature.

For example, if you want a new job where you earn more money and work with people who respect you and your talents, but you believe that you don't have the right education or experience, or that this type of job is not possible for you, it won't happen. It can't happen because while you are saying you want a better job, your beliefs do not support that possibility for you. They are not aligned with it. And there is a lot of fear around this belief, which is a very dense, low level energy.

And you can't put the energy into your life to allow it to happen if your beliefs and thoughts are not supporting the changes you wish to make.

The same principle applies to relationships. If you want a loving, fulfilling relationship but don't believe that this can happen for you, you will not be able to create one no matter how much you try.

And if your thoughts are reminding you of every relationship you had that didn't work, of every person who betrayed you, or that you don't know anyone who has a good, loving and committed relationship so how could that possibly happen for you, you will be frustrated and not see the results you want.

Your mind is a busy machine with an endless memory of everything you have ever said or done or that has ever been said or done to you. In fact, the mind does not think new thoughts; it simply picks an existing thought that closely matches the situation at hand based on its memory of a similar past experience.

When we transform our thinking we are changing our thought patterns and must give the mind some new thoughts to put into its memory.

If we don't, a vacuum is created and the mind will fill it with the first available, similar thought from the past.

Your thoughts and beliefs are the fuel that drives your miracles forward. And each of them has a specific energetic vibration. The Universe hears and responds to the energetic vibration of our thoughts and beliefs, not the words we speak. Unless we raise the vibration of our thoughts, by affirming our power and shifting our beliefs to align with our miracles, what we create reflects the thoughts with the lowest and most dense vibration, which is also our most powerful energetic vibration.

Without the proper fuel, in the form of life-affirming, powerful thoughts and beliefs, which work together to create the vibrational energy that supports your miracles, you will want to create one thing but something else will manifest, something that reflects your actual thoughts and beliefs.

This is why it is important to review your Miracle List every day so you can focus on your miracles and give your mind some new thoughts to fill the vacuum that is being created by your focus on the changes you wish to make in your life and in your thinking.

~~~~~~~~~~~~~~~~~~~

Roger's story: Roger enrolled in Miracle Coaching because his business was failing and he wanted to turn it around. Everything went well at first and Roger progressed through the first few lessons until we arrived at the lesson on beliefs. Then he began to hesitate and nearly stopped the program. Roger had a secret that he kept from everyone and it was the reason that he could not succeed in his business. In fact, it was the reason that everything in his life failed after a certain point.

Roger's father had gone to prison for embezzling money when Roger was a teenager. From that moment, everything in Roger's life fell apart. His parents divorced, his mother had to go to work, they lost their home and had to move to another area. Money was tight and their lives were very difficult. Roger was embarrassed about his father's imprisonment and suffered from the criticism and judgment of his father that he heard from others.

Roger believed that he did not deserve to be successful, that he was a bad person, and that eventually everyone would find out about what his father had done and assume he would be just like his father. Once he was able to face his fears about his family history and acknowledge how traumatic the experience had been for him, acknowledge his guilt and shame and release them, he could examine his beliefs about the situation and work on changing them.

Roger's energy shifted on the day he was willing to release his fears and shame, and he felt like an enormous weight had been removed from his shoulders. And that is what happened, because once he was no longer weighed down by his fears and beliefs, Roger was free to build his business and enjoy the success he deserved.

~~~~~~~~~~~~~~~~~

Exercise: Today, for each miracle on your list, write down why you believe or think it can't happen. In order to release the thoughts and beliefs that are limiting you, you must know what they are. Many of them are unconscious and you are not aware they exist until you are willing to uncover them.

Don't think too much about what you are writing, just write a belief or thought that you have about your miracles about why you think you can or cannot create them. What you write may surprise you but now that you know what your beliefs and thoughts are, you understand why your miracles may have not happened yet. As you continue with your lessons in this program you will be able to raise the vibration of your thoughts so they correspond to the miracles you are creating.

Jennifer Hoffman

Day 5 The Money Trap

We have been taught to believe that without money we cannot have a happy, successful and fulfilling life. We are bombarded with images of what people with money do—take exotic vacations, live in fancy homes, drive nice cars, and purchase beautiful things. So we believe that money is the key to a lifestyle that is beyond what we experience in our daily life, or usually in that of anyone we know. And since we don't have the amount of money we believe this lifestyle requires, we think that we are unable to create the life of our dreams.

But miracles and money are not related, and miracles often do not require money. In fact, money itself has no meaning. We give it whatever meaning it has, but it is really just pieces of paper and bits of metal. How is that possible? Doesn't it take money to buy a nice house, take exotic vacations or live the life that we want? Sometimes, but not always. Many clients I have worked with created miracles that did not require money. In fact, some of them were blessed with exactly what they wanted and also received money or they received their miracles and money was not involved.

Remember my Miracle Story of the free trip to France that I was paid to go on? I did not receive the money to pay for the trip. I was given the trip and didn't have to pay for anything. In fact, I was even paid to go on the trip!

Exercise: Stop here for a moment and write down what you would do if you had an unlimited amount of money available to you. Would you tour the world, start a business, fulfill an ambition like learning to fly an airplane or climb Mt. Everest? Would you buy your dream house or complete your education? Write down everything that you would do if you had an unlimited amount of money. Remember to keep this about you, and not what you would do for others, including your family, children, and friends. Be bold, daring, and decadent as you write down what you would do for yourself, in your life, with an unlimited amount of money.

Now, let's go back to the money trap discussion. Since we believe that it takes money to live our dream life, we stop the process of creating it before we ever begin. Because when we believe that everything we want requires more money than we have as the first step towards its fulfillment, we stop believing in the possibility of our miracles as soon as we begin to focus on them because we can't imagine where the money will come from.

But the Universe often doesn't give us money in response to our requests for a miracle. Sometimes the miracle just arrives and it is a gift from someone else. Or, and this is important, it is actually the answer to someone else's prayer.

The new car that you wish you had could be the car that someone needs a miracle to get rid of. They may be willing to give it to you, sell it for very little or offer a long term payment plan.

Or the house that you want could be one that someone needs to find a buyer for and is asking the Universe at this moment to please send someone who wants the house. They may be willing to allow you to live there free of charge or negotiate on the price or give you very generous terms.

In order to create miracles we must stop believing that living the life of our dreams takes money and if we don't have money, we can't have the life we want to live. Once we begin living from a position of power we quickly discover that money is just energy. Like all energy, we attract what matches what we are putting out, according to our own vibrations. So if we believe that living the life of our dreams takes money and we don't believe that we have or ever will have the money that this requires, we prevent the Universe from helping to connect us with what we are asking for because the Universe doesn't need money to help us create our miracles.

When we believe that miracles happen miraculously (remember they are simply a shift in energy from one place to another), they will appear in miraculous ways.

To start your life on its miracle path, get yourself out of the money trap, the belief that money is the source of the good in your life. Once you realize that money isn't the source of getting what you want in life, and sometimes is not even involved in that process, you open the door to the limitless miraculous possibilities that the Universe has for you.

Rose's story: Rose and her husband took the Miracle Coaching program together because they were buying their first home and were very frustrated with the experience. They had been looking at houses for months without finding one that they could afford and were very disillusioned. As we began the program it was clear that money was an important issue. They did not want to overextend themselves financially and their focus was on how much money they would have to spend instead of on getting the house they wanted. They had found a neighborhood they loved and every house they looked at was out of their price range. They felt they should be looking somewhere else but had their hearts set on this neighborhood and were hoping that something they could afford would be available one day.

Our first focus was on their beliefs about money and both Rose and her husband had experienced some financial limitations as children and were afraid to be without money. They also believed that money had to be saved, protected, was difficult to come by, and could disappear at any moment. Once those issues were addressed we could focus on the issue of the house because while buying a house was something they wanted to do, it was also a difficult step for them to take because of their fears of not having enough money.

I advised them to look at houses in their favorite neighborhood, meet with real estate agents and focus on manifesting their dream house without worrying about how much it was going to cost. They met with a real estate agent who showed them several homes and promised to let them know if anything became available. Several weeks later they were able to purchased a home in their desired neighborhood, which the owners needed to sell immediately, at less than the market price. The house was everything they wanted -- it was in their desired area and within their budget. They were able to find their dream home once they stopped focusing on the money and their fears and were open to receiving their home in a miraculous way—which they did.

~~~~~~~~~~~~~~~~~~~~

Exercise: As you read through your Miracle List today, do you have beliefs about the role that money plays in any of them?

Write them down next to each miracle that you think requires money for its fulfillment (or next to all of them, if you think they all require money).

Do you think that if you had more money you would have the possibility for more miracles or that they would be easier to create?

Today's lesson also included an exercise that asked you to describe your 'dream life', the life you would have if you had an unlimited amount of money. Can you see similarities between what you wrote and your miracle list? Are there any similarities or is your Miracle List limited by your beliefs about money?

Money may play a role in manifesting your miracles, but it is not the only way they will come to you. So as you work on your miracle list today, release any thoughts about how much money will be required for its fulfillment, your current financial status, or how the miracle, or the money, will arrive.

Focus on the miracles you want to create and let the Universe surprise you with its ability to create miracles without money. If you need extra proof that this is possible, re-read Jennifer's Miracle Story at the beginning of the book.

Day 6 The Victim Trap

Do you feel like a victim in your life?

Do bad things always seem to happen to you?

Do you never get ahead, no matter how hard you try?

Do you think that you were born under an unlucky star because nothing in your life ever goes right?

If that's how you feel about your life, then you are a victim. And do you know what? As long as you maintain these beliefs you may continue to be a victim for a long time.

In fact, as long as you believe this, nothing in your life will ever change. You will get the same kind of life, every day, day in and day out, week after week, month after month, year after year. Whatever you believe is what you will receive in life. Nothing more. And all of it will reflect your victim thinking.

Because you believe that you are a victim. You probably tell everyone you know and a few people that you do not know, about how bad your life is, its terrible circumstances, and how nothing goes right. Each new disaster becomes another opportunity to share your misery. And these people agree with you and they sympathize because their lives are in a terrible state as well. In fact, they may be victims too.

But the worst part of the victim trap is that miracles don't happen to people who are victims. Since we create miracles from a place where we are powerful, if we are always feeling powerless because we are always feeling victimized, we can't step into the energy that will bring our miracles to life. And that can make us feel even more like a victim.

When our life circumstances go from bad to worse we feel like a victim and that keeps us in the victim cycle. We feel trapped, unable to move forward and then we tell everyone we know how bad things are and we feel even more like a victim. Until we stop feeling, acting, thinking, and talking like a victim, our situation will never get better. Remember that our reality is a mirror of our thoughts and beliefs, and they are our most powerful miracle tools.

What kinds of words are you using to describe your reality?

Will they help to create the miracles that you desire or do you use them to repeat your victim story?

It's hard to be positive when life seems to be spinning out of control. But to stop the spinning we must first stop spinning or victim story which is creating our reality and that allows s to escape from the victim trap.

Since everything in our reality is an illusion, created from our thoughts, beliefs and words, to change our reality, we must first change our thoughts, beliefs and words, which then moves the energy to change the illusion of our reality. That is usually the opposite of what we want but it can be done and it takes practice.

We must learn to watch our thoughts and words, catching ourselves when we say or think things like 'it will never work,' 'I'll never be able to have that', or 'nothing ever works for me.' Because each time we use words like can't, don't, never, or won't, we're putting ourselves back into the victim trap.

And that blocks the flow of miracles.

~~~~~~~~~~~~~~~~~~~~~~~~

Lynn's story: Lynn wanted to end her marriage and took the Miracle Coaching program to gain the courage to do so. Her husband was emotionally abusive and had been mistreating Lynn for many years. She had very little self confidence, was very scared, and did not have the courage to take the steps she knew were necessary to start a new life.

As we discussed the lessons in our weekly sessions, Lynn's responses to my questions and her homework reflected her victim consciousness. She often used the words "I can't" and spent some time each session telling me how bad her situation was, the latest things her husband had done to her, or the mean things he had said.

When it came time to discuss victim consciousness and the inner voice/outer voice exercises, Lynn found it so difficult that she could not do the homework by herself, so we completed it together. She was able to identify the victim patterns in her life and also see where she had learned them from her family, who were also very enmeshed in a variety of victim stories. As Lynn paid attention to her words and thoughts, she noticed that she spent much of her time reminding herself and others of her victim situation. She also realized how powerless it made her feel and how depressing it was to maintain the constant focus on how bad her life was.

Lynn also realized that she felt empowered by the sympathy she felt from those she shared her victim story with. We addressed this issue by discussing new sources of empowerment she could create, to replace those she would lose when she stop using her victim story.

As she focused on having a 'victor' mentality, she was able to release the victim patterns and gain clarity about her situation. Lynn was able to begin planning her future with confidence and clarity that allowed her to be excited about the possibilities and the miracles that she could now envision for herself and her new life.

~~~~~~~~~~~~~~~~~~~

Exercise: As you read your Miracle List today, are you reminded of how bad your situation is or how impossible it seems?

Is there a victim story from your childhood, or a time when you were disappointed, betrayed or mistreated by someone?

Is there a victim story that is shared by many of your family members? Write down a victim thought or story that is related to any of the miracles on your list.

Do you hear yourself saying that you can't do this, it won't ever happen or it is impossible?

Many things may have happened in your life but they are from your past. They do not have to continue to define your present reality. Remember that everything you want is possible for you and when you are aware that you are thinking and speaking like a victim, change your thoughts and words to reflect your 'victor' mentality.

Monitor your words for the next seven days. Pay attention to the words that you use to describe yourself and your life.

How many times do you use words like can't, don't, never, or won't?

How many times do you tell people how bad your situation is?

How far into the victim trap have you fallen?

You can get yourself out of the victim trap by understanding how powerful your thoughts and words are and how you can use them to change your reality. What you will discover is that as you begin to monitor your words, you will use the limiting words, like can't, don't, won't or never, much less often.

Have you empowered yourself with the sympathy you receive from people when you share your victim story?

What can you use to replace this source of empowerment when you decide to share a more powerful aspect of your life and your self with others?

Once you shift into 'victor' mode, you will begin to pay attention to how often you limit yourself by thinking and saying that your life will never get any better. By replacing limiting words with more positive words and thoughts like 'I am,' I have, I will' you will begin to see your miracles happen in your life and you can share the story of your victories with others instead of seeking their sympathy for your victim stories.

Jennifer Hoffman

Day 7 Using Your Miracle Voice

The most important miracle tool that we have to create our reality is our voice. Our voice has an energy that can literally move mountains. It can create or destroy, depending on how we use it. And we have two voices, an inner voice and an outer voice. Our outer voice speaks about what we want or wish we had in our reality. Our inner voice either supports our outer voice or argues with it.

When our inner voice is supportive and in agreement with our outer voice, our thoughts and words are in balance and in harmony. If not, our inner voice reminds us of all of the reasons that miracles cannot happen.

What would we look like if our inner voice actually spoke aloud?

Would we be proud of or embarrassed by what it said?

What if we used our inner voice to speak about our dreams instead of our outer voice?

Would we be able to convince anyone, including ourselves, that we had the power to make our dreams a reality?

Your inner voice is the voice of your fears and of your past, reminding you of former disappointments, hurts, and pain. It reminds you of how many times you tried and failed, of the people who did not believe in you, of the times you felt less than perfect and of the people and situations that confirm and support your failures and imperfection, now or in the past.

Your inner voice may not even belong to you—it may be an unconscious reminder of the negative comments, judgments, and criticisms that you have received from other people in your life. It may be the voice of your obligations, the things that you believe you should and must do. Your inner voice hears and remembers each negative comment and message and believes them to be true. After all, they often came from people whose opinions mattered to you, so they must be true. Sometimes they originated with the people you thought loved and valued you the most, and that gave them extra energy and importance so you really thought they were true.

When we are on the miracle path we learn to speak with our miracle voice, which is created when our inner and outer voices are in agreement. When these two voices are in balance we are giving ourselves the same positive, uplifting messages on the inside as we are on the outside. It is difficult to stay focused on what we say we want with our outer voice, if there is an inner voice telling us that there is no way things can happen as we want them to. Or that we don't deserve them or are not worthy of them. Or that no one else believes in us and won't support us.

When your miracle voice is active, you say what you want with your outer voice and your inner voice says 'yes.' When the two are in balance and work together, there is as much support for your dreams on the inside as there is on the outside.

Your miracle voice exists in the present moment. It is the voice that claims your dreams as yours, that reminds you that when you co-create with the Universe anything and everything is possible.

Your miracle voice is the voice of your Soul reminding you that you are the embodiment of perfection and that everything on your Miracle List is possible. It talks about your dreams in positive, uplifting ways and uses words like I can, I have, I do, I will and I am.

Your inner voice, when balanced with your outer voice awakens the creative spirit within you and offers support and confirmation that you can create the reality of your dreams and live a miraculous, miracle-filled life.

~~~~~~~~~~~~~~~~~~~~

Ray's story: Ray was frustrated with his life because he was unable to create consistent success. No matter what he did, it would go well for a while and then begin to fail. He felt that Miracle Coaching would provide him with answers he needed to create the success and joy he wanted in his life.

From the first coaching session, it was obvious that Ray's inner voice and outer voice were out of balance. As we discussed his Miracle List, Ray's comments always included something like 'I can't do that' or 'I know it won't happen', or the one he used most often, 'I will never'. So our initial focus was to inventory the words he used as he talked about himself and his life and I counted them during our sessions.

Ray was shocked to learn that he used self-defeating, negative words in every sentence, usually more than once in a sentence. Their use had become such a habit that he was completely unaware of how quickly he destroyed every one of his dreams before he even started.

Ray admitted that his inner voice was one he had heard many times as a child, from his father, who criticized and found fault with everything he did. Ray could acknowledge that his father was reacting from his own failures and disappointments, and was probably trying to protect Ray from failure. He was doing it by discouraging Ray from trying anything new, instead of encouraging and supporting him in his endeavors.

Getting his inner and outer voices in balance was a big relief to Ray, who was happy that he could live without the constant struggle of wanting to do something and then hearing all of the reasons why it could not happen. By the time he was finished with the Miracle Coaching program, Ray had several ideas for new businesses he wanted to start and was excited about their prospects. He even had detailed plans for how to make that happen, and used his fault-finding ability to find all of the potential problems in a situation to come up with a list of potential failures and solutions for each one. His inner and outer voices were now in balance and he knew that anything was now possible for him.

~~~~~~~~~~~~~~~~~~~~

Exercise: Take an inventory of the dialogue between your inner and outer voices as you review your Miracle List today. Your inventory could look something like this:

When my *outer voice* says 'I want a new job where I earn a comfortable income and work with people who honor and respect me',

My *inner voice* says.... 'that's impossible', 'you'll never do that', 'you can't get a new job now because the economy is bad'—or whatever your inner voice tells you.

When my *outer voice* says 'I want a relationship with someone who cherishes me',

My *inner voice* says.... 'you will never find someone like that' or 'all the good people are married' or 'you're too old to find someone like that' or whatever your inner voice tells you.

For each miracle on your list, write down what your inner and outer voice say to you about it.

Your outer voice is the one that expresses the desire for the miracle; your inner voice may be limiting it in some way by bringing up reasons that it cannot happen. Or, it may support your miracles and if it does, write that down too!

Finding those areas where your inner and outer voices are out of balance will help you recognize and eliminate the negative messages that your inner voice is feeding you and bring the two voices into balance. Then, when your outer voice says 'I have a new job where I earn a comfortable income and work with people who honor and respect me', your inner voice says 'Yes, let's create that' and fills you with ideas and the confidence to make that happen.

When the two voices are in balance you are open to perfect synchronicity which is what miracles are all about, when your intention and spiritual nature are working in balance and your life flows in harmony with the abundance, joy and success the Universe has for you in the form of your miracles.

Hint: Tell No One

Learning to create miracles provides us with the ability to manifest our life based on what we want. This provides us with many opportunities to manifest change and create miracles in our life. Each success is very exciting and makes the process easier. It is something that we may want to share with others, so that they can learn to apply the same process in their lives. So, we start the miracle manifestation process and then tell everyone we know, hoping that by sharing our experience with them, they too will be able to understand how the process works and to put it in action in their own lives.

And when we tell them what we are doing they may respond with 'why are you doing that' or 'that will never happen' or 'you're just wasting your time.' Then we can question our motives, possibilities and even doubt ourselves. And, if we have been waiting for the manifestation of our miracles to occur and nothing happens or it happens very slowly or in a much different way than we had anticipated, we believe that they are right and we are doing the 'wrong' thing. We went from excited to hopeless in one short conversation.

How did that happen?

Manifesting miracles is a new life paradigm for many of us, one which requires that we alter every belief system that has limited us in the past. This requires a great deal of faith and trust in our own abilities and in our connection to the Universe. So when we set our intention for change, we want to share the news of our efforts with others. But we are quite likely sharing information with the same people who are part of our old, limiting belief systems.

While they may not deliberately and consciously sabotage our efforts, they can act as a mirror of everything, including all of our fears, that we are trying to move beyond. Instead of cheering us on, they can respond with doubt or bring up our fears and anxieties. Through them we can even hear what our inner voice is telling us. Then we may question what we are doing. And we often take these messages as a sign that we're moving in the wrong direction, especially if the messages are being spoken by people we know and trust.

As we learn to create new paradigms for our reality, we are going against the flow of our belief systems and everything that we have learned during the course of our life. And that includes the beliefs of our families and friends. They will reflect all of our doubts and fears about our intentions back to us, creating the possibility that we will not get what we desire. All they are doing is showing us everything that has been or could be holding us back from manifesting our intention for a miraculous life. We can argue with them but they are not able to see the possibilities that we do. They may not understand that it is not necessary for us to justify what we want to create in our life—we can have it simply because we want it and have asked for it.

So as you create your intentions for your new miracle-filled reality, try to resist the temptation to share your miracles with others until you are comfortable with the process. They will see the proof of your abilities once your miracles have manifested for you. Then they will be asking you how they can replicate your results in their lives. Until that time, know that your intentions for your miraculous life are between you and the Universe and you have all of the power that you need to create miracles and the life of your dreams.

Jennifer Hoffman

Part Two: Setting the Foundation

Another aspect of creating miracles is to establish a foundation of beliefs, perceptions and attitudes that will move us into that vibration where we believe in our miracles and know that they are possible for us. Our outer reality is simply a mirror of our inner reality.

Every thought we have is manifested in our life, without exception.

Every word that we speak has energy that manifests in our life, without exception.

Every belief that we have about ourselves, about others, about the world, and about the Universe is created in our reality, without exception.

In the first seven days you took an inventory of your reality as it is at this moment. You discovered that what have you been thinking, saying, and believing that has contributed to and created the life you are now living. This is how powerful we are. If we do not believe that we are powerful, deserving, and capable of having an abundance of miracles in our lives, they will not be available to us. Changing our reality requires that we change our thoughts so that our outer reality is a true reflection of our heart's desires, free from the limitations imposed by our fears.

This section will help create the foundation of beliefs that will help you create a reality that matches the desires of your heart and reflects the miracles you want to create.

Jennifer Hoffman

Day 8 Moving Beyond Fear

Fear puts a wall between you and your spiritual core and stops miracles from occurring in your life. It is a wall that your soul cannot transcend and that no force or power in the Universe, even your spirit guides and angels, can remove. When you are operating in fear, you are out of the vibration of unconditional love, the source of your power and of your miracles. Fear is the most dense, lowest vibrating energy that you can be in and is the opposite of the most powerful energy of the Universe, unconditional love. Unconditional love is the highest vibrating energy in the Universe and has no judgments, doubts or expectations and it is the only vibration that you can be in when you create miracles.

When you live in fear, any kind of fear, you are living a powerless life. Your circumstances cause you to feel powerless, you become afraid, which leads you to feel more powerless, and you become even more afraid. This becomes a self-perpetuating cycle that manifests in your life as a lack of prosperity, joy, peace, and love, which causes you to feel powerless, which brings in more fear, and so the cycle continues.

There are many aspects to fear. One can be the fear of failure or of success, the fear of not being able to move forward, the fear of rejection, disappointment, or disapproval. We can have a fear of not being good enough or of being too good. We can fear not being liked or valued, or being too popular and having too much responsibility. Often your fears do not even belong to you—you are just experiencing and manifesting the fears of others, including those of your family, friends, and what you have experienced during the course of your lifetime and in past lives. Have you considered that some of your fears, especially the most powerful, confusing, and irrational ones, come from other lifetimes that you do not remember?

The mind stores the memory of what we have learned to be afraid of, so what we fear has its basis in the past. We can only be afraid of something that has already happened, so all of our fear is based in the past. While we project that into the future, it is an illusion because it has not happened yet. Our mind does this to protect us and to prevent us from repeating past painful experiences. But if we are not aware of what these fears are and how they manifest in our life, they can quickly become what prevents us from moving forward, instead of what prevents us from hurting ourselves in this moment.

Our fears can extend to being afraid of having too much—our friends and family may not like us any more, or we may be persecuted by jealous people (this is often a past life memory), or of not having enough over the long term and we won't be able to maintain our life-style.

We can be afraid of what might happen in the future and limit what we do in the present moment out of a fear of re-creating the past. Many of us are afraid to ask for what we want because we are afraid of being disappointed if it does not happen.

Some people believe that they have a limited number of miracles available to them and are afraid to ask for too many. We can even be afraid to ask for what we want because we believe that we have only one choice and are afraid to make the wrong one.

How do you know that you are operating in fear?

Go inside and look at your feelings.

Do you feel disconnected and stuck, confused, hurt, or angry?

Can you feel the panic rise as you read your list of miracles and wonder whether they will happen or what will happen to you if they don't materialize?

Are you afraid of what may happen if they do?

That is your fear speaking and it limits you to protect you from harm. Although it may seem very strong, its power is limited to what you allow it to have. Releasing fear is part of bringing the inner and outer voices into balance and creating your miracle voice, which moves you forward into miracle creation.

～～～～～～～～～～～～～～～

Marta's story: Marta was excited about the Miracle Coaching program and had a long list of miracles she wanted to create, but nearly all of them were miracles she wanted to create for others. I reminded her that everyone has to create their own miracles and even those who are sick and could use a miracle for better health needed to do that for themselves.

Marta had a difficult time accepting this and it did not take long for her fear of being alone, without her family, to reveal itself. Marta had spent much of her life taking care of others and she wanted to ensure that her family would be healthy and successful so that they would be in her life for many years to come.

One of the first things we did was to find the source of her fears and then work on releasing them. Marta's fear story began with her mother's death when she was ten years old, after which she was shuttled between various relatives who didn't really want her but who felt obligated to take care of her. Marta said that she never felt safe, secure, wanted or loved after her mother's death, so having her children and close family around her gave her the sense of security that allowed her to feel safe and loved and she was willing to do almost anything to make that possible. This was one reason she had limited the expansion of her life and was struggling with some career decisions at the time, because of the demands they had that would take her away from her family.

Considering her life experiences, Marta also struggled to understand how each person creates their life powerfully, especially if they are in poor health, have financial problems, or other life challenges. She learned that her fear of being without her family was limiting her potential and options, as much of her time and energy were spent either worrying about or physically caring for family members.

Marta was able to re-create her Miracle List so that it reflected the miracles she wanted to create in her life and for herself. Then she was able to consider using her own time and energy resources to focus on her own goals and create a life that she wanted to live.

And by acknowledging that everyone in her life was responsible for their own reality, she could see them as powerful and this would help them learn to create their own miracles.

~~~~~~~~~~~~~~~~~~~~~~

Exercise: For each miracle in your list, complete this phrase:
With this miracle,

I am afraid that _____

Or I am afraid of _____

To release this fear, ask yourself what it means to you, how you have experienced it before and what you need to heal in order to allow it to leave your consciousness. Be calm in the face of your fear and you will receive the information that you need to heal and release yourself from it.

When you consider your fears, they may seem silly, unfounded, or even embarrassing. But they have been part of your life for a long time and it is now time to release them so they no longer interfere with your ability to create the life of your dreams, so you can walk the miracle path free of the fears that have been limiting you. Remember that what you are afraid of will manifest itself in your life simply because you are focusing on it and empowering it with your energy. And it carries a very dense, low level energy signature that attracts energy to it.

Whatever you fear, especially your strong fears, is going to manifest in your life, instead of your miracles.

Jennifer Hoffman

Day 9 Aligning the Past

Sometimes, no matter how much we try, we cannot seem to make our life situation change for the better. We can focus our intention, say the right words, pay attention to our negative thinking, be grateful for our situation (no matter how difficult it is), but the changes that we want to manifest simply do not appear. And we seem to be repeating past patterns instead of moving in new directions.

Are we doing something wrong?

Are we asking for the wrong things?

Do we just have to live with the situation and accept that it will never change?

The answer to these questions is 'no' and what we are experiencing is a reminder of our past coming up for review and release, and presenting us with a chance to align ourselves energetically with the changes we are making in the present moment.

Any time we try to change what we do, how we act or how or what we think, we will encounter a period where we re-visit the past.

Then we are reminded of every disappointment and failure we once experienced there. It's not a sign that we are doing the wrong thing---it's actually an indication that we are moving in the right direction.

But we have to align the past with the present and reconcile our memories of the past with our desire for transformation. We are being shown what has stood in our way for a long time, perhaps our entire lifetime. After all, something has been standing in our way or we would already have what we want and be living in our miracles!

On Day 2 you were reminded that you are always successful. Until you were ready to transform your thinking, you did not find anything wrong with your life. Even if you were repeating the past, that was fine with you.

But your opinion of the past changes when you ready for something else. However, judging your past and its choices only makes you feel bad and changes nothing. And when you judge it, the past it becomes a gigantic mountain that stands in your way instead of being what it can be, a stepping stone to a different life path, and a reminder to use your power in the present moment in new ways that serve you and what you want to create today.

In the past you may have unconsciously chosen fear, distractions, self-sabotage, controlling the outcome, and an inability to let go of past pain to explain why you could not create miracles. Each of these represents a memory of a painful or difficult experience you had at some point in your life.

When this happens we unconsciously go into self-protection mode to prevent a replay of anything that is remotely connected to that experience, which happens whenever we try to do something new or different. And we will avoid any experience that will create an opportunity to repeat the pain that we have experienced in the past.

The past represents all of the choices you once made. The present moment holds the potential for all of the new and different possibilities that are available to you. The future will be created from your choice to be in the past or in the present. You can choose to live in one timeline or the other, the past or the present, but not both. Everything that stands in your way (or that you believe stands in your way) is an example of something that you are afraid or unsure of, based on what happened in the past.

Rather than allowing it to stop us, we can see the past as something that once existed to protect us and an aspect of our life experience that we can now choose to leave behind because we no longer need it. Identifying what is in our way by understanding our fears from the past is an important part of our miracle process. After all, once we know what something is, we no longer have to fear it.

Unless you consciously change them, your thoughts exist in the past. Your mind does not think new thoughts; it tries to match each new experience with an available memory or thought it is already familiar with. As you change your thinking your mind gets confused and wants to go back to the past. That is why it is important to remind yourself of the miracles you want to create on a daily basis, because your mind needs time to make your new thoughts part of its thinking process and constant reminding of the new thoughts and beliefs you want to create, to support your miracles.

As you consider the choices you made in the past, do they include the things that you 'can't', 'won't' or will 'never' do again?

How do your past choices manifest in your reality again and again?

Do they cause you to do things like engaging in negative self-talk, choosing the same relationships, jobs, partnerships, over and over again?

What do they prevent you from doing, for example, is there something that you would really like to do but can't seem to get started or if you do start, you can't finish it?

Is there something you can't force yourself to do even though you really want to achieve the results you know will manifest from it?

Then explore the purpose behind these fears, where they came from and why they have been helpful to you until now. They are there, after all, to protect you from future pain. And as you set your intention to create miracles you are providing your mind with new thoughts to consider as you create a new, miraculous reality.

~~~~~~~~~~~~~~~~~~~~~

Diane's story: Diane was very clear about her reasons for enrolling in Miracle Coaching, she wanted to create a long term romantic relationship. In fact, she wanted to find her soulmate and was tired of waiting for him. Her Miracle List was focused on what she wanted in her perfect partner and relationship.

As we began the lesson about aligning the past, Diane revealed her sad relationship history. But there one relationship was that I pointed out to her, one that she had not mentioned, which was her first relationship in high school. She had loved a young man but he had betrayed her, in a very public and humiliating way. When she acknowledged that relationship and the pain that she had felt when it happened, and the anger and hurt she still carried, more than thirty years later, Diane could see a pattern in her relationships and how she had always chosen men who hurt or betrayed her, in the same way she experienced in high school. Or, she chose partners that she was not fully committed to, as a way of protecting herself from the potential for pain in the future

With that knowledge about the past, she was able to release the pain and focus on connecting with a partner who would honor, cherish, and love her. The rejection, betrayal and hurt that were part of the past represented a fear and a form of self protection that she no longer needed to bring to the present because she was ready to release her fear of being betrayed, humiliated, and hurt. And Diane's story does have a happy ending as she did find the partner she wanted and is now happily married.

~~~~~~~~~~~~~~~~~~~~~

Exercise: For each of the miracles on your Miracle List, write down one or two events, situations or experiences from the past that you believe block their manifestation.

Or, you could write down some positive, joyful events that encourage you to stay on course and support their manifestation.

For example, if you have asked for a new relationship, what was your previous relationship like?

Was it fulfilling and joyful or were you betrayed by someone's thoughtlessness, criticism, or infidelity?

When you know what is blocking your miracles, you know what you need to change in your thoughts and beliefs to help them manifest?

Are you ready and willing to transform your old thinking, related to the past, knowing that without it you are vulnerable to experiencing real joy and fulfillment, without pain and chaos?

Look at the role the past plays in your life and consider whether there is a connection with your being unable, until now, to manifest the miracles that you want to create. As soon as you are willing to release the past you can begin living in the present moment, which is where miracles happen.

Day 10 Forgiveness

'Forgive and forget' is an adage that we hear often and we believe that if we forgive someone then we must forget what has happened between us and move on as though nothing had happened. For some, this is enough to prevent them from forgiving someone who was the source of trauma or pain.

But this is not an accurate definition of forgiveness. The act of forgiveness is something that we do for ourselves, not for someone else. Forgiveness is about energy and releasing energetic connections, and does not mean that we will forget what happened to us. There are things that we always remember but we do not have to also carry their energy around us. We forgive so that we can move on, heal from and change our own life experiences, and release ourselves from the past.

And until we can forgive everyone unconditionally, we are unable to fully step into our power and create miracles.

We can forgive someone when we realize that their behavior is not about us, it is about them and the fears and limitations that they project to the outside world. It is only our karmic tie with them, and the fact that we have shared lessons and energetic connections which created the scenario for our painful experiences with them.

While we can forgive, we do not forget what happened and we will probably never forget. But we must remove the energetic connection of the memory, which we feel and express in the form of our emotions, where we re-live the pain, and that is the purpose of forgiveness -- to clear our energy field. Forgiveness allows us to detach energetically and emotionally, to disconnect from the anger, fear, and any other emotional energy that the interaction caused us and allows us to remember from a place of energetic detachment, without re-experiencing the incident over and over again.

How do we forgive someone who has hurt, traumatized, betrayed, or physically, emotionally, mentally, or spiritually damaged us? Some people have done the unforgivable to us—but is anything unforgivable in the eyes of God?

The opposite of forgiveness is resentment, derived from the French word *ressentir,* which means 'to feel again'. When we are not willing to forgive someone we are in the energy of resentment, which means that we are willing to feel that situation and to be in is energy, over and over again.

We resent the person who hurt us and want them to apologize, ask us for forgiveness, and give us closure. We want to understand their motivations, their purpose behind causing us so much pain. Without this closure we resent them and what they did. Every time we see them or think about them, these feelings come up again and again and we go through the same emotional cycle. These feelings keep us in a cycle of anger and resentment (feeling again) whose only release is forgiveness.

Forgiveness is a challenging aspect of our spiritual journey because it requires that we transcend emotion and view life from a different perspective, one that acknowledges our power in the face of some of our most powerless and disempowering life situations, and our responsibility, which is more difficult to do. How can we be responsible for these terrible things that happened to us? To explain that, we have to view life from the perspective of karma, soul contracts, and soul connections, to see all of our connections as energy exchanges and to transcend our emotion-based life view. I explain this in great detail in my book, *Ascending into Miracles -- The Path of Spiritual Mastery.* Our inability to do this allows us to continue down the karmic path.

Forgiveness is the way we end karma, achieve our own closure and release ourselves from our pain.

When you forgive someone you do two things: you recognize the lesson they have to teach you and you release yourself and them from the lifetimes of experiences that you have had together and which this lesson was a central focus of. Within these lifetimes, each of you has been both victim and aggressor, the abuser and the abused, playing out a difficult struggle whose only resolution is through forgiveness.

All it takes is for one person to say 'stop', which happens when we forgive, and the cycle of karma, resentment and pain is over. Before you can learn to manifest miracles in your life, it is important to forgive each person who has ever hurt you, no matter how big or small the transgression.

This does not mean that what they did was right, just, fair, honorable, or respectful. It simply means that you are forever releasing yourself from this experience, and the legacy of its energy and its pain, as well as not engaging in resentment so you do not have to feel this again. You cannot move forward into miraculous living carrying the weight of the past with you.

Forgiveness must be unconditional—we cannot attach any expectations or demands to our act of forgiveness, nor must we anticipate any kind of acknowledgement or reward from the other person for our forgiveness. Although that may happen, it cannot be something that we expect, want or hope for.

It must also be complete—once we forgive, the karmic cycle is completed and we have cut all emotional and energetic cords and ties to it and it is over and finished, forever. We cannot bring it up again for if we do, then we must go through the process of forgiveness again, until we can view that person and/or situation from a position of complete detachment and neutrality.

Forgiveness can be done privately, where we make a decision within our hearts to forgive this person or situation and release our karmic connection, or openly, where we discuss our choice and intention to forgive with the person in question. Either way, we are complete with our forgiveness work when we can satisfy its two conditions, that it must be both unconditional and complete.

How do we forgive someone? There is no set formula or procedure and the way in which it is accomplished is up to the individual. We can forgive both the living and those who have passed on. One forgiveness exercise that I suggest to my clients is to write a letter detailing the hurt, pain, anger and frustration that you feel about the situation and the person or people involved. Be as general or as specific as you need to be.

Then write what you are forgiving the other person for and remember to forgive yourself for it too, because you are part of the process. Remember that we are each responsible for all of the details and events in our life.

Once the letter is completed, and the process may take several hours or days, read the letter aloud to yourself and then burn it. These are two very symbolic acts—reading the letter aloud sets the energy and intention for forgiveness and fire is cleansing and healing.

Sometimes this exercise may have to be completed several times, especially if there is a lot to forgive.

How long it takes and what we have to do to forgive is not important; the important thing is that we forgive everyone, for everything, and heal our karma with them. And that removes some serious obstacles to the effortless, graceful and easy flow of our miracles.

~~~~~~~~~~~~~~~~~~~~

Rosemary's story: Rosemary was interested in the Miracle Coaching program because she was at a crossroads in her life and wanted to make some significant changes. She was proud of her recent accomplishments that included obtaining a graduate degree and starting a new job. But she had noticed that there was a cycle of drama and chaos in her life, which she didn't want to experience now. To have her life flow more smoothly, with helpful, positive and supportive people, was on her Miracle List. The first part of the program went well until we reached the lesson on forgiveness.

Then Rosemary realized that the block to the energy flow in her life, which she experienced as chaos and drama, because she could not forgive certain people. She felt that what they had done was unforgivable and that if she forgave them she would also have to approve of what they did to her. And she was unwilling to do that. Even after we talked about how the drama and chaos in her life were reflections of the anger and resentment she felt towards these people in her past, and that if she wanted to attract helpful, positive and supportive people she would have to release the anger, she simply could not consider forgiveness at that time.

In fact, she felt so strongly about it that she did something few people do, she stopped the program and would not continue. Even though I explained to her that forgiveness was about closure and release and did not mean anything else, she refused to continue. Since forgiveness is an important aspect of shifting our energy so we can allow miracles to happen, we could not continue if Rosemary refused to do the forgiveness work.

Although her anger was blocking joy and other things from manifesting in her life, it was a source of power for Rosemary and until she was willing to replace her anger with another source of empowerment, she would be unable, and indeed, unwilling to forgive the people she was angry with.

Exercise: As you review your Miracle List today is there someone or something that you can forgive to give yourself closure and peace?

Is there someone you feel has done the unforgivable and you resent them and their actions?

Does this anger make you feel powerful or fuels your desire to show them you can succeed and have survived in spite of their actions? Anger can be a source of empowerment, although it is not a very powerful or beneficial one. Sometimes we need to acknowledge our use of anger in this way, so we can create a new source of empowerment when we release the anger.

Make a list of people who have done things to you that you consider to be unforgivable, and the list can be short or long. You can write down what they did, if you like, as this list is for your personal use and you do not have to show it to anyone. Once you have written them all down, go back over your list and highlight or place a checkmark next to the ones you are ready to forgive them now.

Then write a letter detailing your feelings towards them, including how you feel about what they did to you and how it has impacted your life today. Be sure to describe your anger in detail because it is what you are willing to release when you forgive them. You can write an individual letter to each person or write a group letter. Once the letter is written, read it aloud and then burn it (or you can tear it up and bury the pieces, or do whatever you feel gives you the closure you need).

Recognize that there may be some people you are not yet ready to forgive. Continue to add their name to the list each time you do this exercise, until you are ready to forgive them.

You can do your forgiveness exercise several times over the course of days, months or even years. When you are ready to forgive someone, you will. Do not judge yourself for what you cannot forgive. Simply realize that it is an experience that you are not yet ready to release and you will do it when you are ready.

Day 11 Life is Perception

Everything in life is as we think it is. The reality that we live in is completely based on what we think it should be because we create our reality from what we know is true -- about ourselves, who we are, what we are capable of, and what we deserve. We will never have more than what we believe is possible for us. If our reality does not meet our needs, it is not because there is not enough to go around or not enough for us, it is because our perceptions about ourselves and what is possible are not in synch with or aligned with what we want.

There is nothing that we cannot have or cannot do but we have to believe in those possibilities. And to do that we must change our perceptions.

Our life experiences are the foundation that we create our perceptions from. When our experiences are difficult and painful we see life as a series of disappointments and failures.

And then we create a life that is disappointing and painful, full of experiences and people who mirror our perceptions and beliefs about disappointment and pain.

Remember that we are responsible for creating our reality and the Universe never gives us more or less than what we ask for. And whatever we ask for is affected by our perceptions. So if we don't have what we want it's not because we don't deserve or can't have it; it's because our perceptions are getting in the way.

To change our perceptions we must review the beliefs that we have about ourselves and the world, and transform those that are limiting, powerless, and negative, to ones that are self-affirming, expansive, positive, joyful, and powerful.

Once we transform our beliefs, we transform the thoughts that those beliefs create and this transforms the energy we are using to create our reality. Most of these thoughts are part of our daily mind chatter, the unconscious and endless stream of thoughts that fill our mind every moment of every day.

Without conscious awareness and intention, our thoughts reflect our negative, self-limiting beliefs. Affirmations are a powerful way to transform our beliefs because they train the mind to think in new and different ways. Here are some affirmations to help you step into a new perception of yourself:

I am a powerful person and capable of transforming anything and everything about my reality now.

I willingly accept responsibility for every aspect of my reality and by doing this, I now willingly accept the power to change it.

I am in charge of every aspect of my reality and I now create a reality that brings me joy, peace, abundance, and fulfillment in every way.

Every day I embrace my power, my divinity, and my creative abilities to transform my life into an effortless, miraculous journey of joy, abundance, and unconditional love.

John's story: John is a multimillionaire and easily creates miracles in his life. In fact, he has the kind of life that most people envy, his businesses are very successful, he owns several homes, takes exotic vacations, and has a 'jet set' lifestyle. But John was very unhappy and hoped that Miracle Coaching would help him find the satisfaction that everyone thought he had. As we discussed his perceptions it was clear that John's past played an important role in his life. His life had not always been easy and as a child he had known great poverty. Money was, for him, a source of survival and confirmation of his power. But he could never have enough and was always afraid of losing his money.

As John worked on separating his beliefs about his own, internal power from the power that he believed his money gave him, he was able to shift his perceptions about what money meant and how he earned it. John admitted that his business dealings were not always honest and he regretted that he was a difficult person to do business with as he was so focused on winning and being ahead of everyone else that he often compromised his principles.

It was difficult for him to turn down business deals, even if they were not always ethical because he was afraid of losing money. And he had to learn to accept that he could take time to relax and enjoy what he had and not continually seek more. We created some affirmations to help him clear his beliefs about money and power and to create a foundation for joy in his life. He learned to define happiness in a new way and to create new beliefs about what made him a powerful person. And he was able to explore ways to help others by sharing his money in powerful ways that supported them on their journey and provided many opportunities for growth and education in his community.

~~~~~~~~~~~~~~~~~~~~

Exercise: As you review your Miracle List today, write down any perceptions or beliefs you have that either support or interfere with your miracles.

Are there times when you feel less powerful, depressed or begin to think about how terrible your life is or has been in the past?

Do these past experiences create fears about the present that control your beliefs and actions today?

Affirmations can help change those thoughts. Use your affirmations every day to create new, more powerful and fulfilling ways for your mind to think about the past and the present. Once you begin, you will be surprised at how quickly you can change your perceptions and create miracles in your life.

Remember to include your miracles in your affirmations. Remind yourself that you deserve and can have every miracle you included on your list. Miracles occur because we are focused on what we want, not on what we don't have, or what hasn't arrived yet. Because your miracles represent what you want, they have to connect with you.

Keep your focus on what you want and avoid getting sidetracked or distracted by your old perceptions.

Day 12 You Have Everything You Need

Every day we are told that we would be happy if we had more--more money, more stuff, more success. This causes us to believe that we never have enough because there is always something else that can make us happier than we are right now. So we constantly feel that our joy and satisfaction will happen with the next step. Then we continue to try to get more of something else to fulfill our needs and be happy. But we always have everything we need, at every moment of our lives because what we have at any moment is what we thought we needed and created at that moment in time.

Yes, even though you may not have everything you want, or what you have right now may not be exactly what you want, you have everything you need. Because you created it and it was created based on what you needed at the time you brought it into your life.

Whatever circumstances exist in your life at this moment, they are there because you put them there. They may have entered your life at a time when you believed they would bring you joy, solve a problem or make you feel better about yourself. Or you may have created a situation because you felt you needed to be rescued, saved, valued, or loved.

They may have entered your life at a time when you weren't paying attention or gave your power away to someone and you now find yourself in circumstances where you feel out of control. Whatever you did in the past was what you needed at that time and now you are ready for something else.

The drama in our life fulfills a need for drama; the chaos fulfills a need for chaos; the pain fulfills a need for pain, just as the presence of joy, love and peace fulfill a need for those things. We may not consciously invite all of those things into our lives, but if we believe that this is what we need, we will unconsciously create circumstances that invite them so we can full those needs. Everything in our life fulfills a purpose. That purpose may be to help us learn a lesson, satisfy a desire, fulfill a dream or gain understanding about who we are and clarity on what we really want—or don't want.

Since everything fulfills a purpose and we create our reality, we always have what we need. Even our most difficult experiences fulfill a need and have lessons to teach us. When we open ourselves up to believing that we can create other options, our needs change and then we can create another kind of reality.

When we are ready to change what we need in our life we can change what we invite into our reality. Eventually we arrive at a place where we no longer need chaos, drama and pain, if we intend and choose to create a life that does not include them. Once we see the connection between how our needs are met by our experiences, we can understand that if we need pain, we get pain. If we need joy, we get joy. If we need peace, we get peace. If we need abundance, we get abundance. And when we are ready to release one need, another need can replace it.

That process of release and replacement happens when we are ready for it, and not before.

As you look at the energy in your life, what do you see as the most predominant energy?

What do you need more of in your life?

What do you need less of in your life?

How do your miracles fulfill your needs?

~~~~~~~~~~~~~~~~~~~~~~~

Lillian's story: Lillian called me to schedule Miracle Coaching and told me that she was doing it secretly and did not want her husband to know. Lillian revealed that she was having an affair and was feeling very guilty about it but was not able to end it. In fact, it was not her first affair, she had already had several in her marriage. She knew that she was putting her marriage at risk and did not know why she was willing to do that.

We focused on why Lillian was willing to engage in behavior that compromised her life and created so much drama. She recognized that she needed and even enjoyed the extra attention she received from the affairs and although she felt guilty, she could not stop herself from pursuing them.

As we worked together, Lillian had an interesting realization about her needs. She saw that she was afraid her needs would not be met by her husband and that he would reject her. She was more comfortable with seeking fulfillment from others, with whom she did not have an emotional connection, rather than having that discussion with him.

She talked about how she had felt unloved and unwanted as a child, with no one to meet her needs. For Lillian, the fear of rejection was so strong that she was afraid to ask someone whose love she valued to address her needs. And yet, she also felt so undeserving and unworthy of her husband's love that she was willing to put it all at risk by having affairs which she knew he would find out about one day. and would possibly reject her for. She recognized that the drama she created in her life reflected the insecurities and fears that had been created in her childhood.

Once she was willing to release the fear of rejection she was able to focus on her relationship with herself and to begin to acknowledge her need for love and attention. She worked hard to affirm that she deserved to have the loving relationship she wanted with her husband and to become more willing to trust him and his love for her so she could release her self sabotaging behaviors. Then she began to do things that brought her joy, including painting, something she had a gift for.

As Lillian made peace with her needs and began the process of learning how to create fulfillment in her life, she stopped creating drama, and could reconnect with her husband without fear of rejection. She also stopped having affairs and focused on more positive, fulfilling behavior, and learned to find the joy and peace she truly wanted with the man who had always loved her as she wanted to be loved, but was unable to accept it from him before.

~~~~~~~~~~~~~~~~~~~

Exercise: Your Miracle List represents a new dimension of living for you, where you are able to be honest about your needs and fulfill them. Review your miracle list and consider the new needs you have set in place with them. You can complete this sentence to help you with that process:

Although I created _____

that   fulfilled my need for _____

I am now creating _____

to fulfill my need for _____.

Here is an example of how this could be completed:

Although I created the job I now have that fulfilled my need to have a steady income, I am now creating the possibility of a new job to fulfill my need to be valued by my employer, to be appreciated for my gifts, and to do work that I am passionate about.

Can you see that what you have in your life at this moment fulfilled your needs until you wanted (and were ready for) something else?

Your Miracle List represents a process of transformation into a new way of thinking and being where you take responsibility for your needs and manifest according to what you want in your life now.

You create new possibilities for miracles when you are ready to expand your thinking about what you need, deserve and can have.

Jennifer Hoffman

Day 13 Expect Nothing and Gain Everything

Our expectations include everything we 'know' will happen, 'believe' is possible and will occur in predictable ways, based on our past experiences. They can protect us from repeating behavior that may hurt us, but they may also prevent us from exploring new opportunities that can expand our life in new and different ways. We put expectations in place with everything we do and when they are not met we have to stop, reconsider our options, and change our path.

For example, if you get into your car to go to work in the morning, you have an expectation that it will start. Or if you take a bus, our expectation is that the bus will be there on time. If those expectations are not met you have to find alternate means of transportation and the flow of your life is interrupted.

You may be upset, frustrated and angry with the situation and feel that it is unfair. But what is really happening?

Do you like your job?

Are you happy to go to work every day?

Are you satisfied and fulfilled with your life?

Your car not starting may be a strong message to you that some situations in your life are limiting you and that there are other possibilities available to you if you can release your fears that block you from pursuing them.

Closely related to our expectations are the attachments that we have, to situations, people, and outcomes. Using the example above, you may be attached to your job because it pays well or you like the people you work with. Or you don't think you will be able to find another job if you quit or lose this one, even if you do not like it.

Our attachments and expectations can tell us a lot about our fears, doubts and insecurities. They often remind us to not make changes, to stay where we are and accept what we have instead of looking for something else. And they let us know where our fears are and how they create situations in our life.

We can be attached to a situation because of an expectation that we are not capable of creating something more fulfilling, so we stay where we are even if we are not happy or fulfilled. We can even expect that things won't happen for us, won't work out or won't be right because they never have in the past.

The problem is not in the process, it is in our expectations and attachments because it is the energy they generate which creates the outcomes we experience. And when we have expectations about situations and outcomes we create boundaries that limit our possibilities and this almost ensures that the past will be repeated in the present. We get everything when we can expect nothing, while holding the belief that anything is possible.

If we have been unaware of our expectations and attachments, they appear when we commit to creating a miraculous life. They are present in the messages we receive from our inner voice, in our thoughts and beliefs, and are mirrored to us in the conversations we have with others.

Our attachments reveal themselves as we begin to consider making changes and we can suddenly find many reasons to stay with a job, to reconsider leaving a relationship or starting a new one, cancel a move or major transformation, or commit to creating miracles. Our attachment to the security, comfort, and familiarity of our existing life is never stronger than when we are trying to change it.

At their most basic level, our expectations reflect our fears and our need to be in control and to feel powerful. Our attachments reflect our need to be loved, valued and appreciated and what we are willing to do and to accept to fill those needs.

And we will try many things to have our needs met in the best way possible. But intertwined within them is the memory of the past, our level of self-worth, how much we believe we deserve to have what we want, and our willingness to be open to limitless possibilities, or our fear of change.

When we can expect nothing and release our attachments we don't need answers to the logical questions about miracles.

How can we get a new house if we don't have any money?

How can we get a new job when we don't have the time to look for one or don't believe we have the right skills or experience to get the job we really want?

Or when we hear that the economy is bad and jobs are in short supply, wouldn't it be foolish to leave the job we have and look for another one?

How can we create a fulfilling relationship when we haven't been able to do that before or when our past is full of sad relationship memories?

The Universe tells us to take care of the 'what' and it will take care of the 'how'. It's not our job to concern ourselves with or worry about how things will work out. The Universe really does work in strange and miraculous ways (if you don't believe me, re-read the story of Jennifer's Miracle Story and her free trip to France at the beginning of this book) and can bring things to us in ways that we would never consider or believe possible. But first we must get to the point where we expect nothing.

We can definitely expect that we will receive the miracles we want but we should have no expectations about how that process will work. Once you set your intentions for your miracles you create a space for them to happen and they will, and in ways that may surprise you. Your new job may be offered to you through a chance encounter, you could be given a new car, or you could be introduced to a new partner that you have an instant connection with.

How will that happen and will it be what you wanted?

It will when you are open to the possibility that something greater than what you can imagine is always possible for you.

Our expectations are based on what we believe is possible based on our previous experience. And we cannot know any more than what we have already experienced. These expectations create boundaries that limit our potential by   directing the energy we move when we set intentions or create miracles, to fit within those boundaries.

And with every thought and word we send out a message to the Universe that says 'help me create this but make it happen 'this' way.' What we don't realize is that we are already dissatisfied with what is happening and we are looking for something else. But until we are willing to release our expectations of what an outcome could, should and will be, we will not allow any new or different potentials into our reality.

When we can control our expectations so that we expect nothing we put ourselves in the flow of the Universal energy and then we can receive everything. It is a powerful place to be, that requires a great deal of trust and faith.

Being in the flow is where miracles happen, things come to us 'out of the blue' and we are in the right place at the right time, connecting with the right people and situations, and allowing miracles to happen in the most miraculous ways. It takes faith and trust to let go of our expectations and attachments and allow the Universe to do its work, but that is what we must do if we are to step powerfully and confidently into the realm of the miraculous life.

~~~~~~~~~~~~~~~~~

Jason's story: Jason took a leap of faith when he enrolled in Miracle Coaching as he was having financial problems and if the program did not work he could not afford anything else. He was sad, depressed, and desperate, and really needed a miracle, or ten. Jason's financial problems had begun when he had to buy his partner out of their successful business. Then the economy in his area began to fail and he was not earning enough money to meet his expenses. After a few months of low revenues he began to worry about how he was going to keep his business running and meet his personal bills.

Sometime during the middle of his program Jason admitted that he was very worried because he did not have enough money to make his house payment that month and did not know what to do. So we made that his homework for the week, that he would see his house payment as being made, to just expect that it would happen in the best way possible without attaching any expectations as to how it would happen. I told Jason that, according to my intuition, it would work out in a very unusual way.

Jason called me the next week and was overjoyed because his house payment had been taken care of, in a very unusual and unexpected way. The bank had experienced a software problem that prevented them from processing payments and had called him to ask him to not send that month's payment. In fact, he did not have to pay it at all, they would put it at the end of his loan. Jason even called them back to confirm that this had really happened with the bank, just to be sure, and they confirmed it.

This event not only helped Jason financially, it confirmed for him that he could indeed create miracles by focusing on what he wanted and releasing his expectations, attachments, and judgments. From that moment forward, Jason had no doubt about his ability to create miracles in his life and that the Universe was capable of delivering them in the most perfect and creative ways, so he was willing to drop his expectations of what was possible and his attachments to the outcome to give the Universe a chance to work its magic.

~~~~~~~~~~~~~~~~~~~~~

Exercise: In today's review of your Miracle List consider your expectations of how they can or cannot happen. This includes beliefs of how they can come to you and any questions or doubts about how they will be created.

Do you understand that every expectation can block your miracles and limit your possibilities?

Are you attached to a situation or people and afraid of how you or they might be affected by the changes you are making?

Your attachments can show you where you are afraid of change and where you are willing to limit your options to meet your needs to be valued, loved and respected, even if you are not receiving those things now.

Write down any expectations you have about each miracle on your list and then re-write that statement in a positive way, knowing that they will happen in the best way possible.

You can even write 'I don't know how this will happen but I know and trust that it will.'

Also include your attachments to people and situations and any fears you have of how those situations may be changed by your miracles.

Remember that when you are willing to create miracles you are seeking new options and are open to the possibilities that everything will work out in the best and most perfect way.

Day 14 Dream Big

When we don't get what we want it isn't because we don't deserve it, it's because we usually don't ask for exactly what we want or don't ask for enough. The Universe has unlimited creative power to grant us our every desire. We just don't ask, or we ask for part of what we want, believing that if we ask for what we really want we're asking for too much.

And then we think that we won't get it so we prepare ourselves to receive much less than what we asked for—remember we already asked for less than what we wanted. So the results often fall short of our desires.

Imagine going to a restaurant and ordering a full meal and then changing your order several times because you think you can't afford a full meal and you finally settle for a glass of water. Well, you could think, you are still hungry but you're no longer thirsty. But you have settled for less than what you wanted and will leave the restaurant hungry, which is why you went there in the first place.

When we agree to accept our power, we must learn to dream big, knowing that we are working in partnership with the Universe. And the Universe is a very big and powerful partner. But the Universe responds to us and gives us what we ask for and are willing to support with our beliefs.

And, if we ask for only part of what we want and don't support that with positively aligned thoughts and beliefs we probably won't get anything at all because what we're asking for is not in synch with our true desires. We must be perfectly honest with the Universe at all times. If we are not, we will know because it will be reflected in the results we manifest.

We are co-creators of our life, working together with the Universe to create the reality of our dreams, which happens through our intention. If we don't dream big enough the Universe is not going to make up the difference. That's not how the process works, although we tend to hope that it does. When we don't dare ask for what we really want, we affirm our lack of faith and our feelings of unworthiness. The Universe works with the creative energy we generate for our miracles. So when we ask for everything we want, the Universe meets us at the point of our desires, reminds us that we are worthy of having everything that we wish, and the result is exactly what we asked for -- no less but sometimes much more.

Our challenge when we create miracles is to dream big enough, to ask for the impossible and to know that it is possible, for nothing is impossible in a limitless Universe. We can ask for exactly what we want and know that it will come to us. We can listen to our heart when it reminds us to ask for what we really want and put the full power of our faith and beliefs behind it. When we dream big we know that we deserve to receive everything we ask for and more.

Do you believe that the Universe has more important things to do than help you with your miracles? That it has more important miracles to create for others? The Universe tells us that it is always with us, watching over us, walking beside us as our co-creative partner. It reminds us that we deserve everything, even the things that we haven't thought of asking for yet. And it also tells us that we can have everything, if we will dream big, ask for exactly what we want, and believe that we can have it. Our big dreams must be accompanied by big thoughts and beliefs.

There is no order of magnitude for miracles, one is not bigger or smaller than another. The Universe has no judgment about our miracles and does not see any one of them as more important than another. Whether we ask for a glass of water because we are thirsty or a new home because we need a place to live, it doesn't matter because all things are equal in the Universe. So we need to dream big because to the Universe, all dreams are big, they all get equal attention and they all get fulfilled in the same way.

Is it hard to identify what you really want, to identify your big dreams? None of us has random desires. Everything that we want is what we wish we had in our lives. Miracles are the voice of our heart, reminding us that there is another, more wonderful potential for our reality and other possibilities for us.

We must learn to dream big, to ask for everything we want and not hold ourselves back. If you could see into the future and know that everything you wrote on your miracle list would come to you, would you have asked for more?

The 'more' is your big dream. Ask for that because it is what you really want. As you continue to work with your list for the rest of the 30

Days to Everyday Miracles program, ask yourself every day if you have the confidence to ask for something that represents a bigger dream. If you do, then write that down because it represents what you really want. The only way we limit the Universe's ability to co-create with us is by not asking for what we really want or by not dreaming big enough.

~~~~~~~~~~~~~~~~~~~~~~

Kyle's story: Kyle was a gifted writer who had writer's block and he hoped the Miracle Coaching program would help him. He was very excited about the program and looked forward to each new lesson. Each one gave him insights into his life and his thoughts, in ways he had not been able to consider before.

With each weekly session Kyle's Miracle List expanded as he became clearer about what he wanted and more willing to consider other possibilities. His breakthrough arrived when we discussed limitations and dreams, as he understood how he had been dreaming 'small' and limiting his ability to write from the heart because he was afraid of rejection.

In his life he had experienced rejection from his family and he had not realized, until we worked together, how hurt he was or how much pain he carried from his past. Once he released this, by understanding that their rejection reflected their own small thinking, he could be open to using the fullest expression of his gift for writing. Then he began to write at a level that surprised him, free of his writer's block and writing more expressively with a greater intensity and focus than he had ever done before. He knew that his big dreams, to become a famous writer, could become a possibility once he allowed himself to dream big.

~~~~~~~~~~~~~~~~~~~~~

Exercise: Look at your list of miracles. Did you ask for what you really wanted?

Is there more that you want? For each item on your list, ask yourself these questions:

Is there more that I want in this area?

Did I dream big enough or did I hold back?

Am I really happy with this miracle or do I want more?

Then re-write your Miracle List, if necessary, so that your list truly reflects everything that you want, and as much of it as you want to receive.

Remember that the Universe can also bless you with a bonus when you have the courage to ask for exactly what you want, so be prepared to receive even more than you asked for.

Jennifer Hoffman

Hint: You Can Do This

When we initiate change we arrive at a point, usually just as the changes are ready to manifest, and decide that we simply can't do it; it's too hard. That feeling comes from the fear that the changes won't happen and we will be disappointed in the outcome. Or we may be feeling alone, scared, and unsure of our ability to follow through. We have nothing to fear because when we are creating miracles, we are never alone.

We have the full force and power of the Universe behind us, willing to help us and cheering us on. It has been waiting for this moment, this opportunity to help us live the life that we came here to live, to step into our miracle mastery.

The life secret that we have not yet learned is that life is not supposed to be hard. It is supposed to flow effortlessly, with miracles occurring at every moment. All we have to do is learn to ask and to be willing to receive the miracles that come our way. So if you are feeling that this has become a very difficult process, that it is 'too hard', remember that you are not doing this alone.

As you review your list of miracles, imagine that there is help coming to you from every angle. And if things get too difficult, ask for help and guidance. You have powerful spiritual resources available to you and willing to be of joyful service to you, but you have to ask them for their help.

Creating miracles is a new and different way of being and thinking, one that we are unfamiliar with. This can create doubt and confusion, until the new way of thinking becomes more familiar. Just continue to move forward and know that you are working towards your miracle goals, which are always within your reach.

And don't forget to pay attention to the miracles that may already be occurring around you. They are there but you must be looking for them. And you won't be able to see them if you're wondering whether you're on the right path, and doing the right thing in the miracle process.

The first part of the process of creating miracles, removing the blocks, and examining your beliefs so that you can change them is exciting. Finally, you think, I'm going to start living the life of my dreams. And you begin to make progress, clearing out old beliefs and even watching some miracles occur.

Then something begins to happen—the old, negative ways of thinking begin to come back and may even seem to be stronger than before. You begin to doubt what you're doing, wonder whether it's worth the effort or whether you can change. And you feel like you have gone backwards.

You have not really gone backwards, you have created a gap in your thinking and your mind, without a firm grasp on your new reality, is struggling to get back to its old, familiar and comfortable routine and thoughts. As long as you stay focused on your goal, creating miracles, it will pass and things will get better. But you must be aware that it may feel, at times, like you're taking a step backwards for every two steps that you take forward. Even if you do that, you're still ahead of where you were before you started.

Remember that we feel comfortable with what's familiar, even if it is not making us happy. Our comfort zone is not where we are comfortable, it is where we are dealing with everything that is known and familiar. Any change takes us from our comfort zone to our discomfort zone.

And the old ways will, from time to time, come up to remind us that they are still a possibility. That is why it is important to review your list of miracles every day, to maintain your focus on the new reality you want to create for yourself and for your life.

Jennifer Hoffman

Part Three: Practicing the Principles

We live in a world that is governed by Universal Law. We tend to think of these laws as encompassing things like gravity—what goes up must come down, the Sun, which always rises in the East and sets in the West. But these are physical laws that govern physical matter. There are also spiritual laws, universal principles that govern both spiritual and physical matter.

These laws are simple and powerful. And they are absolute, meaning that they are what they are, we cannot change them. The Universe is very exacting—there is light and dark, yes and no. We are the ones who look at things in shades of gray and live in a 'maybe' world.

The sum of Universal law is absolute reciprocity, our reality is a reflection of the energy that we are using to create it. Our fear and doubt create those things for us, measure for measure. But, what we give out in faith and love, we get back multiplied many times over. And when our intention is to reconnect with our power, to live in unconditional love and to live the life that we were born to live, without fear, we create miracles. The process is easier when we understand the Universal principles that govern the energy that we are using to create miracles and learn how to use them in positive, powerful, life-affirming ways.

Jennifer Hoffman

Day 15 Surrender or Resistance

Our understanding of surrender is based on the concept of winning and losing, where the winner is the one who succeeds and if not, then they lose. And we believe that it is better to win, whatever that takes, than it is to lose. So we will do all we can to ensure that we win, that we succeed at whatever we try, no matter how hard we have to work at it or how long it takes. Sometimes we try to win just for the sake of winning, because we don't want to lose, even if what we are winning is not that important to us. If we have to surrender, or give up, we have lost and this makes us imperfect and unsuccessful.

But the one who surrenders is not the one who does not win. Rather, the one who surrenders is someone who acknowledges when it is time to stop fighting, to let go of things that are not flowing effortlessly, and to consider focusing their time and energy in other directions. If we are not in a state of surrender then we are in resistance and fighting to either make things happen or allow them to stay the same. Surrendering doesn't make us a 'loser', it makes us wise and very aware of how we are using our energy and what we are empowering with it.

Every experience contains a choice to surrender or to resist. With our 'no pain, no gain' life philosophy we choose the path of resistance and struggle through our lessons, embracing the belief that life is difficult and the most meaningful victories or successes are those that require the most effort.

But life is not about winning, it is about moving forward. When we are not willing to surrender we are attached to a particular outcome, limited by our expectations, blinded by our will and our determination to make things work. Surrender presents an easier option, one that removes obstacles and allows the energy to flow in our life.

Overcoming your lessons, the difficult experiences in your life, is not about winning, is an opportunity for learning, healing, and release. When you are in resistance you want to win and you are driven by your free will, which includes attachment to a particular outcome. Together, these prevent you from seeing all aspects of your lessons, including the release that is required to gain closure. This also prevents you from moving to a higher perspective where there is an option to surrender and allow the energy to flow in the direction it needs to go for release, healing, and peace, as well as success. When you surrender you allow your self-love to guide you into the flow of miracles.

Miracles require that we understand our power of co-creation, where we work with the Universe to create the reality of our dreams. When we are not willing to surrender, or to stop fighting, we tend to believe that the Universe is blocking us when life gets too hard or things don't work out as we expect them to.

Instead, we are being directed to stop resisting, to stop pushing against the energy that is trying to move us in a different, possibly more fulfilling, graceful direction, but we're resisting this option or possibility. Surrender allows us to be open to other options and to the knowledge that there may be another solution to our situation, one that is outside of our current perspective or level of understanding.

Every situation where you have to work hard, struggle and persist, where you feel threatened and overwhelmed, is an invitation to try surrender, to let go of the need to win and the fear of losing, and step into effortlessness. If not, then you are resisting, pushing against the forces that offer you the peace you are seeking and the real victory that you want.

The path of surrender is the path of least resistance, where we step into the flow of Universal energy, where we are at one with our purpose and learn our lessons without creating more hardship for ourselves. There are two paths in every lesson and life situation, with options of surrender or resistance. Both will get us to the same destination and deliver somewhat similar results but the path of surrender may offer a more pleasant, shorter, and more fulfilling journey to a destination we may not have considered.

The path of surrender and effortlessness is available when we are able to release our belief that resistance yields more rewards or victory is more meaningful after a struggle.

We choose the path of least resistance, or the path of surrender when we are in a state of detachment, without expectations of the outcome and free from the baggage of the past. Then we can be at peace with our lessons, accept 'what is' and acknowledge the blessings that are inherent within everything. To see this path we must be out of fear and into its higher energy, that of unconditional love.

When we remove our emotional responses and their associated feelings of anger, disappointment, hurt, unmet expectations, and sadness, all of our lessons take on new meaning. They become opportunities for learning instead of proof that we are not good enough, unlovable, unworthy, or undeserving of what we want. And then we can find peace because within the path of least resistance there is peace instead of chaos, freedom instead of pain, and joy instead of sadness.

Within each lesson is a choice point, a moment where we can choose the path of surrender or that of resistance. When we are emotionally charged the choice is not obvious but it is there. And we can always change our choice. Nothing, except our pride and our pain, says that we have to see a difficult lesson through to the bitter end, which often means 'win at any cost'.

Once we realize that there is an easier, less painful and difficult way we can stop and simply move on to an easier path. That takes detachment because we have to be willing to accept, stop resisting, forgive, be willing to see another path, and surrender. That's hard to do when we are on a mission, we want to be vindicated and someone has pushed us to our last nerve.

There are questions to ask when making this choice, like:

Do I really want to do this?

How far am I willing to take this?

Why is this so important to me?

Am I willing to let go?

Is there another option available to me in this situation?

Once we understand why we are so vested in winning and in resistance, surrender becomes an option. Of course, if we choose the path of resistance anyway, we will arrive at the same level of learning and growth. But we don't get any additional points or blessings by making our life difficult. It may take a little longer and we may be worn out at the end but we will eventually arrive at the end of the lesson.

The path of surrender is the path of miracle creation, where we learn to stop fighting the flow when life becomes difficult, learn our lessons without sacrificing our peace and joy, and take the effortless path in every situation because we don't get extra blessings for making our life difficult.

~~~~~~~~~~~~~~~~~~~~

Brenda's story: Brenda enrolled in Miracle Coaching because she wanted help with a relationship. She loved her partner and wanted to do all she could to help the relationship become committed and long term. But there were problems and Brenda thought a miracle would help.

One of Brenda's miracles on her Miracle List was that her partner learn to appreciate her and the efforts she was making to keep the relationship moving forward. I reminded her that she could not ask for miracles on behalf of someone else. She could ask for a loving, committed relationship but not for something that forced another person to behave in a certain way. And by being very specific about wanting a relationship with that person, she was trying to control the outcome, which was blocking her miracles. I asked her to consider was why she was willing to work so hard at maintaining this relationship and why she was resisting the possibility that it could end.

When we reached the topic of surrender and acceptance, Brenda realized that she was resisting the truth about this relationship and her partner's behavior. She knew she had to accept his behavior and if she could not, then she had to surrender to the potential truth this was not the right relationship for her. Brenda also had to look at why she was taking this so personally, why she was reacting towards what she saw as rejection and trying to 'win' her partner's love and approval without considering whether it was something she really wanted from him, or whether he was capable of giving it to her in the way she wanted to receive from him.

Although it was challenging because she had invested significant time, emotion, and energy in the relationship, Brenda decided to surrender and stop working so hard to keep it alive. It ended shortly thereafter and while Brenda was sad, she knew that by surrendering and releasing it, she could allow a new and different relationship to become possible. Then we explored how she worked so hard to avoid rejection, even in situations where an ending and closure were the best possible options. She had to go back to different periods in her life where she had been disappointed by people, including her family, and resolve some of that pain through release and forgiveness. Then she could learn to ask her assessment questions to ensure that her energy was directed in ways that were aligned with the outcomes she wanted to create. And at the first sign of struggle, she learned to go into surrender mode, to avoid going into resistance and make things work, to stop fighting, and intend the most effortless outcome.

She changed her Miracle List to ask for a relationship with someone who appreciated her and already had the qualities she wanted in a partner. And she did find that person, two months after her Miracle Coaching program ended Brenda connected with the partner she had asked for on her Miracle List and is very happy in her new relationship.

~~~~~~~~~~~~~~~~~~~~~~

Exercise: As you review your Miracle List today, consider the areas where you may be in resistance.

Are there things that you feel must happen and happen in a certain way, and are you willing to do whatever it takes to make them happen?

Are you afraid of what might happen if they don't?

Can you see areas where surrender would put you on the easy path?

Next to each miracle on your list write down one or two beliefs, thoughts, issues, feelings or situations from the past in which you could surrender (which means to stop fighting) to put you on the path of least resistance and to allow your miracles to flow to you.

Do this without judgment, simply allow any areas of resistance to be revealed to you so that you can release them.

You can also explore why you are in resistance, what you think you gain by fighting, or lose if you do not fight, and how you would feel if things were easier or more effortless.

Jennifer Hoffman

Day 16 Life is Effortless

When we interact with the Universal energy in an effortless way, we send energy out in the form of our thoughts, words, and beliefs and the results are manifested in our reality. This is how everything in our life is created, as we consciously or unconsciously manifest the life that reflects who we believe and think we are back to us.

With conscious use of this effortless flow we are fully aware of exactly what we want and that is what we create. With unconscious use of the effortless flow we are sometimes or often surprised at what is happening in our life because things happen unexpectedly and we feel out of control.

At every moment there is a constant energy exchange between us and the Universe where our every desire is fulfilled (on an energetic level) at the moment we think of it. The manifestation in our reality may take a little longer. This effortlessness has nothing to do with being easy, as it is an energy flow with no judgment. It merely responds to us without asking whether this is what we really want or would prefer something else.

Each thought carries equal power. Whether you are worried about the low balance in your bank account or imagining unlimited financial abundance, the Universe uses those thoughts to help you effortlessly manifest what you are thinking about.

No matter what is happening in your life right now, it has been created as an effortless process of bringing your thoughts, beliefs, words, and actions into form, as your reality or the life you are living in each moment.

Do you have a life of ease, an abundance of what you want, joy, love, and peace? Maybe you do or maybe not.

Maybe your life is a constant struggle, where each day you try to make things happen, you work hard at being happy, and struggle to find fulfillment. Some people live by the saying 'No one said that life would be easy'. But who said that? Someone who had a difficult life?

We can believe that life is hard and we can also have the belief that life can be easy. We create ease or an easy life when we understand effortlessness. Effortlessness exists in the Universe and life becomes easy when we learn to work with it in a conscious and deliberate way.

When we understand effortlessness we know that we are working with a powerful energy that is continuously expanding in every direction. And the energy never moves backwards although it may seem to when we repeat lessons and experiences from the past. But the energy follows our intention and as long as we focus our intention in the present moment, our life is expanding in a forward direction and we are creating new potential for our reality that is based on the limitless potential of the present.

When we focus our intention on the past, we bring the past into the present and create our reality from it. Then the energy seems to move backwards but that is not what has happened. We have gone back to the past and the Universe is merely responding to our past-based thoughts and re-creating the past in the present.

Using this energy in a conscious and deliberate way means that we remain focused on the miracles we have asked for and have faith that they are happening, even if they do not seem to manifest as quickly as we would like. We can also use this energy unconsciously when we allow our habitual thinking, negative self talk, doubts, and fear to dominate our thoughts and actions. When we begin working with miracles we are changing our thought patterns and without conscious effort, we will easily revert back to the old, limiting thought patterns that have previously blocked our miracles.

In order to work with effortlessness we must release our need to be in control, our attachments to specific outcomes and our need to know the 'how' and 'when' of every situation. Effortlessness requires faith, the knowing that our requests are always heard and responded to and the results will flow to us in the best and most perfect way possible.

Everything in our life is supposed to flow effortlessly to us. If it does not, it is a sign that we have fears or blocks that we are not consciously aware of. Or we are creating a lesson that we could choose to avoid. Perhaps what we have asked for is not in our Highest Good, or out of integrity with our intention. Or we could be attached to a specific outcome or want to be in control of a situation that we need to release. But we often misinterpret those messages to mean that we must push harder and then we find ourselves putting all of our energy towards getting what we want without considering that there are other, more effortless, and more fulfilling options that will bring us more joy, abundance, love and peace, more of what we have asked for, without so much effort.

With the principle of effortlessness we recognize that when our life is not manifesting in a way that brings us joy, it is time for us to let go of what is not working. Part of understanding effortlessness is recognizing that obstacles steer us away from that which is not in harmony with our Highest Good or our intentions. Being willing to trust in a benevolent Universe that always has our best interests at heart and having faith are other ways we ensure that our life flows effortlessly.

Miracles arrive effortlessly when we stand in the flow of Universal energy and use it consciously to create what we want but are willing to detach from the outcome. If there are things that are not flowing to you effortlessly, let go of them and allow the free movement of energy in your life. Know that whatever you willingly release will always be replaced by something else that will come to you effortlessly because it is fully aligned with your intention.

~~~~~~~~~~~~~~~~~~~

Kate's story: Kate thought Miracle Coaching would help make her life flow more smoothly and that was one of the miracles she wanted to create. Kate had a busy life with a family, children, an active social life, many friends, and a large extended family. She was very involved in the lives of many people and was the matriarch of her family.

When we discussed energy flows and effortlessness, Kate under-stood that this was what she wanted. But when we discussed that she needed to choose a focus for her time and energy, instead of being an integral part of the lives of so many people, Kate hesitated, unsure of how to proceed.

Her breakthrough came when she realized that she enjoyed being a central element in the lives of so many people and the control and the input she had in their lives, which made her feel needed, valued, and important. But she admitted that the neediness she had created in those who depended on her was interfering with her life in many ways. When she was in control she knew how and when things would happen but it also meant that she worked very hard, all of the time. Could she focus on her own needs and still have the appreciation, validation, and attention of her family that were so important to her?

As Kate discovered, the more she was willing to release the need for attention and control, the more effortless her life became and things began to 'fall into place'. A person she wanted to speak to called her first, an appointment she was late for was cancelled, someone gave her a gift of an item she wanted to buy.

She also began to say 'no' to requests for her time and allowed others to do things for her, instead of feeling responsible for everyone else. Kate noticed that as she released her control, her family members began to act with greater confidence and self awareness. Their conversations took on a different tone and energy, and she felt more comfortable and at ease at family gatherings. She also noticed that she had much more free time and was pursuing new hobbies and interests, without worrying who might need her for something. And all of her relationships took on new energy as people saw her less as their advisor and caretaker and more as someone who was interesting and fun to be with. Kate got the value and love she needed, and she was able to let go of her obligations and as she let energy flow effortlessly into her life, her miracles also appeared in the same effortless, easy and flowing manner.

~~~~~~~~~~~~~~~~~~~~

Exercise: Are there some miracles in your list that are not flowing to you effortlessly?

Are you trying to be in control of the process, or have attachments to specific outcomes?

Even though you have asked for a specific miracle, is it possible that another aspect of it is being created, one that you cannot see yet?

Perhaps it is time to let go of the ones that are not manifesting for you and ask for other things.

Or to release control of the process, which includes allowing others to give to you, and invite effortlessness into your life.

If this is the case for you, re-write your Miracle List, removing those miracles that are not flowing effortlessly and replace them with ones that affirm your power and create effortlessness in your life.

Have the courage to ask yourself if this is what you really want and be open to the answer without judgments or expectations.

Expect your miracles to come to you effortlessly, because this represents the conscious and deliberate use of the Universal energy which is always working on your behalf, to help you create your miracles.

Day 17 Live in Gratitude

Gratitude is a state of being and a way in which we connect to our creative power. When we live in gratitude we affirm our power by acknowledging the role we play in creating our reality. Being in gratitude for what we have, who we are, what we are receiving, and are about to receive is the how we create miracles. Living in a state of constant gratitude is how we affirm our connection with our Source and acknowledge our power and our divinity.

Each one of us is a divine, spiritual being. We work through our divinity, which exists at the level of energy, compassion and power, instead of our humanity, which understands and lives through emotion, when we live in a state of gratitude. It is through gratitude that we create transformation because unless we can be grateful for what we already have we are unable to create something else. The lower vibration of gratitude is contempt.

We must be grateful for every experience, every situation, and every person that has participated in every aspect of our life. They have helped bring us to the point where we could recognize and stand in our power. It is through the lessons they participate in with us that we are able to gain the spiritual understanding that enables us to create joy, peace, and unconditional love, and to create miracles.

No matter how difficult or frustrating an experience or person is, they participate in our lessons to help us gain clarity and insight, and to heal our karma. We can release them and ourselves from further interaction, which includes our karma, with a spirit of gratitude. If you think that gratitude means that we have to like everything, that is not the case. Gratitude incorporates acknowledgement, acceptance, detachment, and non-judgment.

Before we were born, we created a plan for our life and the lessons we would learn, we chose the partners who would help us carry out that plan and learn its lessons in the most perfect way. Maybe the lessons were more difficult than we thought they would be and the people more cruel, unkind, and thoughtless than we had anticipated, but the plan was our creation. For it, and its participants, we must be grateful. Without the lessons and their participants we would not be who we are today.

Being in gratitude is also an acknowledgement of our power and taking responsibility for our reality. When we feel that we or others have made mistakes or bad decisions we are in the energy of contempt. With contempt comes blame, shame, guilt, and resentment. Those energies do not contribute to the healing and release of any situation, they keep us in resentment, feeling the energy over and over again as we re-live the past and brings its energies, outcomes, and potentials into the present.

While we may not appreciate the circumstances, we can be grateful that we can view the situation from a different perspective and remember that everything in life is a lesson, an opportunity to learn, heal, and transform. Being grateful for that situation and what we have learned from it allows us to have closure and release it.

We are in contempt, which is the lower energy of gratitude, when we judge all actions, ours included, according to what we think they could or should have done. And we believe they, or we, could have done better. We have contempt for ourselves when we judge ourselves by believing we could or should have made different or better choices.

Peace is possible when we understand that everyone, including us, acts within their highest and greatest potential at all times. They do not have the knowledge or ability to act any differently. Accepting that we experience the best of what someone has to offer to us in every situation, and that we do our best in every situation, releases us from contempt and into gratitude for the role they play in our life.

Take a moment to think about the most difficult person or experience in your life. Do you believe this person could have acted in a different way than they did?

Can you accept that they did the best they could and followed the only path they believed was available to them, no matter how insufficient or inappropriate you think their actions were?

Can you see the lesson that this situation helped you to learn?

Be grateful for that experience and lesson, for what you have learned and the person you have become because of it.

Now release it with gratitude, knowing that once you can be grateful for its presence you can free yourself from it forever.

Can you be grateful for all of your miracles even if you do not see evidence of them in your life at this moment? It is easy to be grateful for our blessings when we have them. Can we also be grateful for them before they arrive, knowing that the energy of gratitude expands their creation and increases the level of effortlessness with which they can flow to us?

Gratitude takes practice, for we have learned to resent the difficult situations and people we encounter on our life path, believing that they are the enemy who hates us and wants to make our life miserable. Unless we can be grateful for everything, without judgment, we keep them close to us because while gratitude blesses us with peace and closure, resentment keeps us in the energy of anger and frustration. If we practice gratitude every day it becomes a habit that allows us to move forward in the flow of the Universal energy.

When we can be grateful for both the small and big things in our lives, the easy and the difficult, the seen and the unseen, we are able to see and acknowledge the beauty of every experience and the synchronicity of how the Universe brings the perfect people and situations together to us to help us fulfill our life plan.

Do you want a difficult situation to be over, a difficult person to change, or to turn a frustrating experience around? Gratitude is the key to accomplishing this. As soon as you express your heartfelt, soulful gratitude for everything in your life, your perspective changes, which then re-directs the energy you are using to empower your challenges into new avenues. Re-directing the energy disempowers the difficulties and empowers new possibilities for your life. This creates room in your life for the miracles you want to create and allows more fulfilling situations to enter your reality.

One more thing here, gratitude is not the same as 'like'. We can be grateful for things we don't like at all. Gratitude is an acknowledgement of the power that we have and use to create our reality. Once we can arrive at a state of gratitude, we can release an experience and make room for something else. We don't have to like it, we just have to acknowledge ourselves as its creator and make a commitment to use our energy in other ways.

Be in gratitude, for all things, so you can be fully on your miracle path and allow the miracles you want to create to flow effortlessly to you.

~~~~~~~~~~~~~~~~~~~

Doug's story: Doug enrolled in Miracle Coaching to help him resolve issues around his divorce. Not only had his wife had an affair and divorced him, but he had just heard that he was going to have to pay her significant monthly alimony payments for several years. He was furious and knew that he had to resolve and release his anger because it was interfering in his life and in his business. But he was so angry at the situation and at himself for being such a fool to have married her, to have stayed married to her, to have thought that she wouldn't try to take all of his money in the divorce, that it had gotten so far out of control, and he needed some help finding new avenues for this energy once he got closure with it.

Doug appreciated the ability to work through some blocks and saw how he had overlooked many issues and problems in his marriage. He also saw how he had contributed to the affairs and the breakdown of his marriage by being physically and emotionally unavailable, as he worked long hours and did not always pay attention to his wife's needs.

But he struggled with the concept of being grateful for the experience. How could he be grateful for the emotional and financial upheaval this situation had put him through?

Doug did agree that the process had made him more aware of what he needed to do to be a better partner in a relationship. And it had made him more focused and driven at work, as he had to rebuild his finances. So I challenged him to practice gratitude and to view the alimony as a tithe in return for the lessons he had learned from the experience. And he was to hand over the first alimony check to his wife, which was due that week, with a big smile and gratitude that he had the means to pay it. His agreed to do that although I know he thought he was going to look foolish.

He could not wait to tell me his news as our next Miracle Coaching session started. The day after he paid his first alimony payment his company received its biggest contract ever and Doug's commission was more than five times the amount of the alimony check. His gratitude had turned his alimony payment into an unexpected payoff. He now hands over every alimony check with a smile and is grateful for the experience with his ex-wife, as it has allowed him to be a much better partner to his new wife.

Doug is very happy with his new life and relationship, and grateful for everything that he experienced which allowed him to create it.

~~~~~~~~~~~~~~~~~~~~~~~

Exercise: There are two parts to today's lesson. First, think about an issue in your life that you are not pleased about, something you think is unfair, unjust, unreasonable, and that you are angry and upset about. Focus as much gratitude as you can on that situation, be grateful for every aspect of it because that is how you are going to create a wonderful blessing from it.

Every time you think of this situation, be grateful for it, especially the aspects you think are the most troublesome, as this is what will shift the energy into something more joyful and fulfilling.

In Part Two of today's exercise, be grateful for every miracle on your list as you review it, whether or not it has happened. Write down everything that has helped bring you to this moment in your life, where you are ready for transformation. Even if you are unhappy, can you be grateful for your unhappiness and see that is one of the reasons you are willing to consider a new path for your life?

Take some time each day to practice gratitude. Find five things to be grateful for each day. At first, try simple things such as being grateful for your home, that you can read this book, your family, your eyesight, or being able to walk. Then gradually move on to things that will take some effort. Remember that once you can be grateful for an experience you will gain closure and release it. Being in gratitude creates the energy that allows our miracles to manifest effortlessly, without resistance.

And don't just pick the good and wonderful things in your life because that is too easy. Be grateful for the things you are not happy about, the things that are inconvenient, uncomfortable, unfortunate and difficult. It is our ability to shine the light in every corner of our lives, which we do with gratitude, that allows us to heal, grow, learn and transform to live a miraculous and miracle-filled.

Day 18 Have Faith

Faith is the belief in things unseen, the knowing of the unknowable as truth, the release from the need to see before we can believe, which blocks the flow of miracles. We must have faith in order to create miracles because we are truly 'creating something out of nothing'. If we think of our dreams as 'castles in the air', then our miracles are what will bring those castles into our everyday reality. Even when the situation appears to be completely impossible, our faith reminds us that nothing is ever impossible, as long as we have the kind of faith in the process that allows us to believe that we are powerful enough to create any reality we wish, even if everything around us doesn't appear to support that belief.

Faith and trust go together and when we have one, we have the other. We cannot trust without having faith and when we have faith, trust automatically follows. When are faced with issues that challenge our faith and trust we must trust in the Universe, as our co-creative partner in our reality, to provide the things we need. We know that what we ask for will be given to us. But are we willing to put our faith to work for us in situations where we cannot clearly see the results, especially when they have not yet manifested?

It is easy to have faith when dealing with tangible elements and processes that have a logical and foreseeable outcome. But what happens when the outcome is unknown? For example, if you are being led to move to a new, unfamiliar place, will your faith allow you to make the move and trust that each experience there is part of your spiritual path and contributes to your spiritual growth? When things do not appear to go well, do you begin to regret your decisions, doubt your faith, believe that you have made a mistake, and that you have lost the Universe's support?

When we begin to create miracles and to believe that they will happen for us, it takes faith to continue to move forward when the miracles do not happen immediately or if they will take our life in new and different directions.

Faith is universal. There is no size or measure of faith, it is not big or small, does not exist in partial or incomplete ways. If you have faith, then you have faith in all things, seen and unseen. Without faith you trust only what you can see as possible, limiting your opportunities to what you know may happen, based on your past experiences. But if you take a 'leap of faith' then you allow yourself to accept the 'unimaginable,' the blessings that are beyond your knowledge and understanding and open yourself to the true unlimited abundance and boundless prosperity of the Universe. Have faith and fly!

With faith you can see the gift in each experience so that it becomes an opportunity for growth and movement instead of fear and doubt. Having faith means that we trust in our infinite creative power, know we are supported by the Universe, and have the ability to create the life of our dreams.

Are you able to trust that if you take a 'leap of faith' that the Universe will help you unfurl your wings or that it will have the net waiting for you? There is only one way to find out—to leap into the unknown with faith and know that your wings are there, waiting for you to use them.

~~~~~~~~~~~~~~~~~~~~

Rita's story: Rita had always wanted to travel to Europe and took the Miracle Coaching program to help her manifest a trip and create some other changes in her life. She wanted to be more trusting, have more faith and to live effortlessly. These are some of the things she put on her Miracle List.

But Rita had learned, throughout her life, to be careful, to distrust, and to not depend on situations or people. This was hard for her to overcome and she received a number of tests that challenged some of her beliefs during the program. Towards the end of the program she still had not manifested her trip and actually had less money than before and was getting a little concerned. So we worked on her focus and intention and having faith, and her homework that week was to simply believe that her miracles were happening.

Rita could not wait until her next session to tell me what had happened so she emailed me her great news. Not only had she manifested the trip and the money to pay for it but she also got a new car. She received a mailer from a car dealership asking whether she would like to trade her car in for a newer model. They would give her a good deal on the new car and a substantial amount for her trade in. At first

Rita did not trust the offer, thinking it was a scam. But she remembered our discussion about having faith and decided to try it anyway.

And she was glad that she did because the new car payments were much less than those on her old car, and the payoff on her old car was enough to pay for the trip, with some left over for spending money. By taking a leap of faith, Rita was able to manifest her miracle trip effortlessly and received something else she wanted, a new car, without even asking for it.

~~~~~~~~~~~~~~~~~

Exercise: As you review your miracle list today, do any of them require a leap of faith? The first leap of faith is your ability to believe that you deserve the miracles you wish to create. If any of your miracles require that you do something that may scare or even terrify you, for you to change your way of thinking and being, then you must find the faith to take the first step.

For each miracle, write down a leap of faith it may require, which may be to change a belief, to take action or to trust that the Universe will work with you to make your miracle happen.

The Universe asks us to be a co-creator in our miracles and all that requires is that we take the first step and believe that we will be provided for. If you are being asked to take a leap of faith it's because you're ready, everything you need is already there, and all you have to do is take the first step.

Day 19 The Present Moment Matters

Everything in the Universe exists in the present moment and there is no concept of the past or the future. While that may seem very complicated, it is quite simple and just means that this moment is all that exists. Whatever happened in the past has led to this moment and whatever happens in the next moment depends on the choices we make in this moment. Although we consider life in terms of yesterday, today, and tomorrow, or past, present, and future, when we work with the Universe and energy, there is only one point in time and that is the present moment. Whatever thoughts and beliefs we have in this moment are the ones that have an effect on what manifests in the next moment.

Where is the present moment? It is the one in which we are breathing. Since we live from one breath to the next, the present moment is where we are taking a breath.

This has two important implications for us in the miracle process. First, the past does not matter. So what you could not create in the past has no bearing on what you can now create in your life. If you had wanted it and could connect to it then, and it would be part of your life today. Remember the past does not exist for the Universe, which operates exclusively in the present moment.

It is the focus on the past that brings it into the present moment, which limits what we create in the present moment to what we were able to create in the past. Think of it this way, if we spend all of our time thinking about what happened in the past, that is what we will create in the present moment.

The Universe never says that we can't have something because we were unable to manifest it in the past. It simply says whatever we want now, in this moment, is available to us now, as long as we ask for it and believe we can have it.

The future does not exist as a place or point in time within the Universe either. So if we are always focused on the future and expecting that our joy will come at some later date, we spend all of our time waiting because what happens in the future depends on what we are doing in the present moment. Whatever we want to have in the future we must create the same intensity of feeling for that in the present moment that we would have in the future. The more positive, excited, and engaged we can be with our miracles in the present moment, the more quickly they will manifest for us.

The other important implication is that we want and can connect to is available to us now. Our beliefs, thoughts and energetic vibrations all affect what we can manifest. When they change, different opportunities and connections become possible. And as we become more accepting of and open to different possibilities we are less concerned with the timing of our manifestation for we know that everything happens at the right and best time. Miracles are a matter of potential, opportunity and timing. And they all meet in the present moment.

Whatever is on your list of miracles is available now. If you have not yet seen the results it is because the process of creation, of bringing all of the elements of your miracles together, is still in the process of manifesting and coming together. Miracles happen with Universal timing, which means they happen at the right and most perfect moment (when the energy, flow, and connections are perfectly aligned) and that is not always when we think they should.

Being in Universal time, not human timing, which requires patience, is another lesson that we will learn as we manifest miracles. Here's a little secret -- patience is nothing more than the process of aligning our will and sense of time and timing with that of the Universe.

~~~~~~~~~~~~~~~~

Joe's story: Joe thought the Miracle Coaching program would fast track him into the life of his dreams. In fact, Joe asked me whether he could do one Miracle Coaching session each day and complete the program in a week, rather than the standard one session each week for eight weeks. We compromised by doing two sessions a week, as long as he could keep up with his reading and homework. Joe had a long list of miracles and was always interested in knowing how he could create them more quickly. As he learned, there was a reason for his impatience.

As we discussed some of Joe's blocks, he remembered that as a child he was always being told to hurry up, go faster, to not take so much time to do things. And as the youngest of ten children, Joe had good reason to learn to do things quickly, especially at the dinner table.

He learned that if he did not eat quickly, someone else would think he was not hungry and take his food. Joe went to bed hungry quite a few times until he learned to eat fast, and that belief translated into other areas of his life. He was always worried that if he wasn't quick enough, someone would take the opportunities away from him. This is the fear that drove Joe to work harder, longer, and do more and do it more quickly than everyone else every day.

Joe was always focused on the future, on what might happen, could happen or was about to happen. He worried about his abilities, his health, the economy, his business, and everything in between. In fact, when he did the inner voice/outer voice exercise he was surprised at how much his negative thinking was present in his everyday thoughts.

His breakthrough came as we were talking about being in the present moment and he realized that he was always living in the past or the future, which was causing him to ignore and miss much of what was going on in his life. He was actually quite successful but once he completed something, he was always moving on to the next thing and found it difficult to enjoy any of his accomplishments.

Joe was able to appreciate his successes once he took the time to write them down, as part of his homework, and reflect on how much he had accomplished. He realized that he did not have to be afraid that someone was going to take his success away from him, that he could stop running towards the future and take some time to enjoy his life in the present moment. At the end of the program, Joe was planning a relaxing vacation, something he had not done in ten years, to celebrate his successes.

Exercise: Have some of your miracles not happened yet?

Are you getting a little nervous and is doubt beginning to creep into your awareness?

Is this causing you to remember the disappointing results you have had in the past?

Whatever you could not do in the past no longer matters; what is important is what is happening in the present moment. Know that the process of manifestation began as soon as you asked for your miracles. When you see the physical results of your materials is not important as long as you have faith and trust, which also helps them manifest more quickly. By not worrying about 'when' they happen, you create the potential for more wonderful and powerful results too.

With today's review of your Miracle List write down any fears about timing you have around your miracles, especially the ones whose outcome is more important to you. How can you release those fears by having more faith and trust, in yourself, in the Universe, and in the process?

Acknowledge your fears, know that they are there and then transform them into positive statements, such as 'I know that this is on its way to me now.'

What can you do to be in the present moment and enjoy and be grateful for the life that you have created up to this moment?

Are you aware of and do you appreciate and acknowledge the success that you have created in your life?

It may help to write down every success you have created in your life, or in the past five or ten years. You may be surprised at how many you have and how much you have actually accomplished.

Then be sure to acknowledge and celebrate yourself for the wonderful things you have done and prepare to create even more wonderful things starting today.

.

Day 20 The Law of Abundance

The Law of Abundance states that we have unlimited abundance in all things, at all times.

We always receive everything we ask for in unlimited abundance.

Every word we speak creates unlimited abundance.

Every thought we think creates unlimited abundance.

And all of this is reflected in our reality. That is how powerful we are. What are you speaking and thinking about right now and what type of abundance is being created in your life?

Whenever we acknowledge our power and perfection, we get more of it in unlimited abundance. When we live in a state of gratitude we receive more things to be grateful for, in unlimited abundance. And everything that we hate, complain about, regret, or feel bad about, we get more of in unlimited abundance. Every time we complain about our life, we get more of what we're complaining about. When we look at our life in terms of what we don't have, we get more of that too.

Each thought and word that we think and speak is amplified through the Law of Abundance.

We live in an abundant Universe and everything in it exists in abundance. An oak tree only needs to produce one acorn every year, yet each oak tree produces thousands of acorns. Each flower produces thousands of seeds and each one will produce many flowers that will in turn produce thousands of new seeds. There are billions of stars in the sky and countless drops of water in the oceans.

Our judgments about abundance cause us to believe that it exists when we have an abundance of what we consider to be 'good' things, such as money, success, joy, and love. Yet abundance exists in all things, even poverty, lack, sorrow, unhappiness, and chaos. Even if we think the law does not work when our abundance consists of problems, lack, and unhappiness, it is always working. As with other Universal laws, it is not judgmental so it merely responds to our vibrations by connecting us with the type of abundance we are creating. When we release our judgments about what abundance includes, because it includes every-thing, we are using the Law of Abundance effectively.

Visualization sets the foundation for the manifestation of abundance, as we cannot create something if we cannot see it as being possible. To use visualization effectively, simply imagine as many aspects of your miracles as you can.

Imagine how you will feel when they appear, your joy in them, imagine what your new house looks like, feel the excitement when driving down the road in your new car, or the closeness of being in your new relationship, or whatever is on your Miracle List.

Extend your visualization to taking action. If you have asked for a new home, visit homes that are for sale. If you want a new car, look at and test drive new cars. Do you want new friends or a relationship? Join organizations whose members share your interests. The Universe is our co-creator, not our magic wand and taking action is an example of our faith and trust as well as creating an abundance of energy that is aligned with our miracles.

Remember that the Law of Abundance works with energy and we have to be in the energy of the kind of abundance we want to create, in order to connect to it. The Universe works with us, not for us, and everything we do that affirms our miracles and moves energy in their direction is both a confirmation of our faith and focuses our attention on the kind of abundance we wish to create. This is why you work with your Miracle List every day, as that maintains your focus on the energy of the abundance you want to create.

As we know more about the Law of Abundance, we realize how easy it is to incorporate it into our life and to get the results that we want. That is 'abundant thinking', knowing that everything comes to us in abundance and intentionally focusing our intention in that direction.

We always receive an abundance of what we think about and ask for, so we can have whatever we want, whenever we want it, and allow ourselves the luxury of living in a state of abundance in wonderful things instead of an abundance of things we wish we had not created.

We can use the Law of Abundance in creating miracles by remembering that there is abundance in all things and focus our intention on the kind of abundance we want to create, which is reflected in our miracles. And what we ask for will come to us in unlimited abundance, so we could receive even more than what we asked for. As long as we remember that there is abundance in all things and stay focused on the kind of abundance we wish to create it will manifest for us in the most perfect, abundant way imaginable.

159

Ada's story: Ada's story was one I often hear from Miracle Coaching clients, she had no money, was suffering from poor health and was not speaking to one of her children. Her Miracle List included improving her finances and health, and creating a better relationship with her daughter. From the beginning, though, Ada struggled with understanding how she had abundantly, powerfully, and successfully created her reality. How could she have created the situation she was currently in? She didn't have abundance, she was broke and sick. According to Ada, that was just not possible. Someone else was responsible but she was not sure who that was.

Then, when it came time to discuss the concept of abundance, she was unable to see how her financial situation and poor health represented the abundance in her life. She knew that if she had abundance, it would involve having a lot of money and great health. It took some time for Ada to acknowledge that she was creating abundance of many things that she did not want in her life by focusing on and constantly complaining about the unhappy situations in her life.

And she recognized that she had a powerful inner voice that was focused on every problem, fear, and doubt from every experience in her past, as well as what was happening to her in the present. In fact, she recognized her inner voice as that of her mother, who spent most of her time complaining about her life. Ada realized that she even used a portion of our coaching sessions to complain about her problems.

This was so upsetting that she had her breakthrough. In preparation for her next session, she had written down everything she had created in abundance, taken responsibility for it, and indicated what she wanted to change. She had also written down every negative, self defeating comment her inner voice used and spent time consciously monitoring her thoughts. She found that during that week, she felt better, worried less, and received some unexpected money as well as a phone call from two of her children.

At the end of the program, Ada was happier, more positive and more focused on creating an abundance of what she wanted in her life.

~~~~~~~~~~~~~~~~~~~

Exercise: When you created your Miracle List you may have thought that what you wrote represented the fulfillment of things you did not have or were missing in your life. Now you know that everything exists in abundance, without classifying it as good or bad, or being enough or not enough. For each miracle on your list, write down how your miracle makes you feel, what you will experience when it manifests and any additional abundance that could come to you. For example, a new job with a higher income might allow you to take a special vacation or purchase your dream home.

There is always abundance in everything and your Miracle List helps you focus your thoughts and intention on the kind of abundance you want to create. Focus your thoughts on your miracles because they represent the abundance that you want in your life. As each of your miracles manifests they add new layers of abundance to your life.

Day 21 The Law of Attraction

Of all the Universal Laws, the Law of Attraction is the most popular and yet the least understood. The Law of Attraction states that we attract people and situations that match our energetic vibrations and mirror our every thought and belief back to us. Everything in our life exists because we have attracted it. The amount of love, peace, and abundance in our life reflects our energetic vibrations we had when we created them. The amount of discord, chaos and lack that we experience also reflects our energetic vibrations at that point in time. And the people and situations that are part of those interactions are connected to us because we attracted them.

The people who betray us, are disrespectful, who do not honor us, the difficulties that we endure, the problems that we have, are all in our life because of the Law of Attraction. But that can also change what we are attracting at any moment. As soon as we make the decision to live our life in a different way, to create miracles, to start living the life of our dreams, and to be in our power, we change our energetic vibration and that changes what we are attracting.

The Law of Attraction also states that when vibrations do not match they repel each other. So when we raise our vibrations, which happens when we acknowledge our power, manifest what we want and transform our way of thinking and being, we repel or disconnect from all of the things that do not match our new vibration. This means that many people, things, and situations may leave our life simply because they are pushed away by our new, different energetic vibrations.

The miracle process will create many changes—we will attract new things to us by virtue of our new vibrations and the old things that no longer resonate with us or match our vibrations will fall away. So as we work with the Law of Attraction it is important to remember that the miracles we are creating will be attracted to us by virtue of our vibrational energy—the more we stay in the flow of energy, the more we stay focused in our miracles, the more we walk in faith and trust, we allow the Law of Attraction to become the magnet that will attract our miracles to us.

~~~~~~~~~~~~~~~~~~

Sally's story: Sally would laugh if she heard me say that she was one of my more challenging Miracle Coaching students, but she would have to agree with me. Sally enrolled in Miracle Coaching because she didn't think she had enough money and wanted to make more, a whole lot more. She was very upfront and honest about her intentions. All of her miracles were focused on making money and what her life would be like if she had more money. I reminded her that she should not ask for money so she amended her list to reflect the financial abundance she wanted to attract.

Sally was not poor but she did not have the financial resources that she wanted or thought she should have. When we discussed the Law of Attraction and how we attract everything in our life, she was confused.

Since she was so focused on attracting and having money, how could she have financial problems? During that part of our discussions she actually became angry with the concept and said that she wanted to be shown what it meant. And she got the confirmation she asked for.

Within a week Sally had several thousand dollars in additional expenses that created even more financial lack. It seemed that every time she talked about attracting money, she received an unexpected bill or expense. Sally began to think that the Miracle Coaching program did not work because her financial problems were getting worse instead of better.

But Sally realized that as she was trying to attract money, she was also focused on what she did not currently have. Each thought she had about attracting financial abundance was accompanied by a thought about her financial lack. Her focus was on what she did not have and she was attracting more of it. So instead of raising her vibrations she was staying in the vibration of financial lack, and attracting many situations that were keeping her locked into a cycle that drained away her money and financial resources.

Once Sally realized this she put her focus on manifesting her miracles and applied faith and trust in the process. Within a short time she was able to create the financial abundance she wanted to pay off her debt and make significant progress on her financial goals that had been part of her Miracle List. This time, though, she was approaching them from a position of abundance, affirming how much she had, whether or not she had it in that moment. She released her fear of not having enough money and instead, focused on attracting all of the resources that would meet her needs and increase her abundance many times over, in any way possible.

~~~~~~~~~~~~~~~~~~~~~~~~~~

Exercise: You work with the Law of Attraction to manifest miracles in your life. Your decision to create the life of your dreams has opened the door to this potential for you and raises your energetic vibrations so that you can attract what you want. Look at your Miracle List and for each one consider what you need to do in order to attract your miracles to you.

Do you need to change the way you think or speak about yourself and your life or situation?

Do you need to be more positive, have more faith and trust, and manage your expectations?

What have you attracted to your life so far and what has been released because your energetic vibrations have changed?

Do you appreciate what you currently have or what you have accomplished in your life? Are you grateful for it and do you acknowledge yourself for all of your successes?

Write down any changes you believe you need to make to use the Law of Attraction effectively to create the miracles on your Miracle List.

Hint: Be Willing

We all have free will and it is our free will that prevents the Universe from stepping in and creating change in our life before we ask for it. The Universe cannot violate our free will, just as we cannot violate anyone else's free will. In the same way that we must sometimes watch our children make mistakes and wait for them to ask us for guidance, so the Universe must watch us struggle until we are willing to set aside our free will, which is often our belief that we are alone and must do everything by ourselves, and ask for help. The principle of free will is one that we all live by. All the Universe needs to help us is for us to be willing to do things different and to create an opening for it to participate in our life.

When we create miracles we tell the Universe that we are willing to set aside our free will to co-create with it, surrender, and allow ourselves to be guided by Spirit and to view life from a different perspective. The power of the Universe is always available to us when we are willing to work at its level, which is the level of miracles and limitless possibilities.

We have examples of this when things seem to go from bad to worse and there is no help in sight, when we turn to God, Source, or the Universe, and ask for help, out of desperation or simply because it is our last resort and we need a miracle, and something miraculous occurs.

It is at our moment of desperation, when we absolutely must have a miracle, that we can set aside our fears and free will by surrendering, which means that we stop fighting, pushing and forcing, and let the Universe help us. At that moment it is no longer important how things happen, we need them to happen right away. Doing things our way, ignoring our spiritual connection and wanting to control the outcome are no longer important. It is when our need for miracles becomes greater than our fear of change, that our greatest miracles occur.

But we do not have to wait until that moment. We can balance our need to express our will and our desire to create miracles by remembering that we work in partnership with the Universe, and it is our constant guide and source of support in every moment. Our need to do things alone, our way, and to work hard for results, ignores our spiritual connection and the ease with which we can manifest what we want in our life.

Creating miracles is how we use the Universal energy and spiritual power to manifest what we want and need in our lives. There is no magic formula, no secret key to this process, all it takes is our willingness to surrender and stop fighting, set aside our free will for co-creative partnership with the Universe, to transform our thinking and accept help and guidance from our spiritual resources. As long as we are willing, we can create miracles every day, in every area of our life.

Part Four: Putting It All Together

By now you may have seen signs of some of your miracles occurring. That is such an awesome part of this process, knowing that you have created a change in your life simply by asking, doing your inner work, perhaps surrendering and releasing, and watching it unfold before your eyes, where you see the results in your reality. Creating miracles is a very simple process that involves asking and receiving.

And it is something that we can use every day of our lives. As with many things, the first time is the most challenging. Each additional miracle becomes easier until manifesting miracles becomes the way we live our life.

We have already discussed setting the foundation, removing the blocks, and described the principles of how the Universal energy works in our lives. The last part of this book discusses how we put the final pieces in place and presents some final topics and ideas that will help make this a lasting process for you. These final elements will help you to understand how to perfect your miracle manifestation and create the life of your dreams, every day of your life.

Jennifer Hoffman

Day 22 The Right Intention

We can have anything that we focus our intention on, as long as our intention is right. How do we know that it is? When we ask for what we want, what is best for us, reflects the desires of our heart and will bring us peace, joy, abundance, and unconditional love. Creating miracles is part of our spiritual journey because it involves many of the spiritual lessons that we came here to learn, such as stepping into and using our power, connecting with Source, working with the Universal energy, allowing ourselves to experience life through our potential, and creating the life that our heart tells us is possible for us. All of these things can be ours, as long as we understand the principle of intention.

Intention is the process of creating a pathway for energy to flow into by envisioning outcome we wish to manifest. Miracles are the result of an intention. We create an intention when we say 'I wish'. An intention is created when we see something and decide we want to have it.

Can you see how powerful this process is and why we should be very conscious and aware of how we use it?

Our intention can come from faith or from fear. When intention comes from faith, we ask for what we want because it is right for us at that moment. We don't wonder whether it is practical or logical, what others will think about it or whether we deserve it. We ask because it is what will bring us joy.

When our intention comes from fear, there is always an element of doubt present within our thoughts. We may create several different scenarios, to prepare ourselves for disappointment, so we have Plan A and Plan B, and maybe even Plans C and D. Or there is a fear that there is not enough and someone will receive our miracle before we will, and there won't be enough for us. With fear we ask for what we think we can get, for what we need to get us out of a problem in the short term, or for far less than what we really want. Our expectations and attachments also reflect our fears and influence our intention.

Misusing intention is a misuse of our power and energy, which will deliver disappointing results. Then we will think that the miracle process does not work. It does, when our intention is aligned with our miracles and not with our fears.

There are several guidelines we must follow when we work with intention. First, what we ask for cannot violate the free will of others. Each of us has the ability to create our own reality and we are each responsible for what our reality looks like. No matter how much we love someone or want to help them, we cannot violate their free will by forcing our intention for a better life, more joy, peace or love, on them. We must be willing to see their life as being perfect for them, no matter what it looks like. Because it is — it is the life that they choose to live and to create for themselves. It's hard to watch those that we love struggle but their struggles reflect their use of power. We cannot violate their free will by trying to use our intention to change their life.

We must honor others' choices even if we do not understand them or they go against what we want. We cannot use our intention to force others to do things on our behalf. We cannot, for example, ask for someone to like or love us, to accept or cherish us. If we are with someone who does not do those things, they have their reasons and it is up to us to decide whether we will move on or wait (within a state of acceptance of who they are and what they are doing) but we cannot use our intention to force them to be or to do what we want.

If our intention is for a loving relationship we must be willing to set the intention and be at the energetic vibration which creates the space for that type of person to enter our life, and to let go of the relationships that do not align with that intention.

If one of the miracles on your miracle list is to heal someone else, your intention is for them and not you, and it violates their free will. People suffer through illness for a variety of reasons which we cannot know because that is part of their spiritual contract and their life path. We cannot bring them to a place of being healed and whole, no matter how much we ask for it because being willing to heal is their decision. We can help them arrive their own decision to heal by being a source of joy, strength, and inspiration.

But we can't do it for them through our intention.

And our intention should focus on what we want, not on creating something that someone else has. We can look at someone else's life and believe that if we had the same things we would be as happy as we think they are. But then we are making assumptions about someone's happiness and success that may not be true. We cannot have another's life, but we can set our intention to create joy, abundance and love in our own life.

Our intention reflects our willingness for transformation, to receive the blessings that are perfect for us, and is effective when we are free of attachments to and judgments about the outcome. When we are attached to an outcome we have expectations about how our miracles will manifest, which often reflect our fears. With judgments we limit ourselves to what we believe is possible. In this way we ignore the greater blessings that may be available to us.

The best use of our intention is to focus on miracles that will bring us joy. If a new car will bring you joy, then ask for a new car. If it's a vacation, then focus on creating a vacation. It doesn't matter if it's practical or logical, for when we start focusing on whether we could or should have something, we are judging ourselves and limiting the flow of energy to us. We also lose track of why we want miracles in the first place. And if our intention is focused on having more than someone else or being better than someone else, we will block the miracle process and flow.

So ask for what you want and remember there is enough for all. And if you need a new job but would really rather go on vacation, ask for both things and create two miracles. Set your intention for the joy you wish to create in your life and the miracles that will allow that to happen.

Miracle manifestation works with the right intention. When we ask for what we want in our lives, focusing on what is best and right for us, we will get everything that we ask for, and more.

~~~~~~~~~~~~~~~~~~~~

Norma's story: Norma's miracle list was focused on helping her family, specifically her husband, who was having serious health problems. Norma hoped that she could help him take better care of his health so they could enjoy their upcoming retirement years together. In our first session we discussed her Miracle List and I pointed out that all of her miracles were for the benefit of others. So she re-wrote her list so it reflected what she wanted to create. This list was much shorter than the first one and I could tell her heart was not in it. Norma really wanted to help others create joy in their lives and she wanted to be a blessing to them.

As we discussed the topic of intention it was hard for Norma to understand that everyone was using their intention in the most powerful way they could. How could someone intentionally create unhappiness or poor health for themselves? Was her husband intentionally creating his bad health and if that was the case, why wasn't he using his intention to create good health. Didn't he love her and want to spend their retirement years together?

Norma was a happy and successful person yet she felt guilty about her success because she believed that the people closest to her were not as successful as she was. It was hard for her to accept that they were using their intention to create lack and were not as interested in creating success as she was.

Norma knew that her husband was unhappy with his stressful job. She eventually acknowledged that his health reflected his unhappiness and that unless he changed his intention for his life he would continue

175

to have poor health. It was his choice and did not reflect his feelings for his wife, although Norma believed that if he loved her, he would take better care of himself.

Instead of trying to change her husband's intention, Norma focused on her intention to have a healthy husband and a fun-filled retirement. Rather than spending time complaining about his health habits, she talked about their future and things they could do together. She began to plan events and do things she enjoyed, instead of waiting for him to take the first step.

As she focused on his good health and having fun, her husband became more interested in his life and his health. He asked Norma to help him with his diet and became more interested in planning for their retirement. Norma realized that by changing the way she expressed her intention and being in the present moment instead of waiting until he felt better to do things, she was able to create exactly what she wanted and have him participate in the process. Now her husband was taking care of his health and they were doing things together. She was able to achieve this without complaining or giving up the things she wanted. Norma learned that while she could not force him to do what she wanted, she was able to create the energy for it by focusing her intention on what she wanted for herself and allow him to change his intention when he was ready to make the change for himself.

Exercise: Today's review of your Miracle List will focus on your intention.

Did you ask on behalf of others in any of your miracles, directly or secretly?

Are you violating anyone's free will, even unintentionally?

Are you asking for things that require others to change their lives for you?

Do you feel joy in your heart when you focus on your miracles?

If not, ask yourself what would bring you joy.

Then modify your Miracle List so that it reflects the best intention you can create in this moment, and that is whatever is best and right for you.

Ask with the right intention and your miracles will flow to you effortlessly.

Jennifer Hoffman

Day 23 You Have the Authority

You are the authority in your life. There is no power in the Universe that has control over you and your life. It is your free will that allows you to choose the reality that you wish to create, just as your free will also allows you to make an unlimited number of life choices. While you can be influenced by others and often are, the final choice in the path that you take is always yours. When you give your authority to others, believing that they know best or that they are more capable of creating what you want, you simply give your power away and even then, they have no authority in your life other than what you allow them to have.

Giving your authority to others puts you in the position of walking on their path, which may not be the best option for you. You cannot adopt another's experience as your own, just as you cannot see the world with the same perspective as anyone else. If you believe that others can make better choices than you can, you are living with the expectation that they will take care of you, make you happy, make you feel better, or bring you success. Have you ever given someone else authority in your life and been unhappy with the results? Or, have you ever given someone else authority, power, and control over you and your life and been happy with the results?

Claiming your authority in your life puts you in the powerful position of being aware that you are always in control of what happens to you and how it happens. Then you can eliminate those people who need or want to usurp your power in order to feel powerful, and resist the temptation to giver your power away. When you know, without question, that you are the authority in your life, you do not need to experience realities where you give your power away. No one can bring more joy, peace, blessings, security, abundance or love to your life than you can. That's why you are learning about miracle creation, because it is how you shift the energy in your life and that happens most efficiently when you know yourself as the authority.

Think of the root of the word 'authority', which is 'author'. An author creates stories and if you consider your life as a story, who do you want to create that story for you? On another level, who do you think can tell your story in the best, most truthful, most powerful way, you or someone else?

You create miracles using the authority that you have to manifest your reality. No one can give you this authority; it is something that you must acknowledge and accept for yourself. Living with the knowledge that you are the authority in your life reminds you that you are in charge and that your reality will unfold as you create it. This is powerful knowledge as it reminds you that you are a co-creator with the Universe—it is your job to ask for what you want and then let the Universe respond accordingly.

This is not a random process—you will always receive exactly what you ask for, according to your intention, faith, and trust. So when you feel tempted to allow someone else to bring you joy, love, acceptance or happiness in exchange for your power, remember that you are the authority in your life.

Do you want to walk on another's path or have someone else control what happens on your path? Remember also that you can only receive as much love, peace, abundance or happiness as you are capable of creating for yourself, as the author of your life story, and the authority in your life.

And that when you create miracles you are using the authority you have to create joy, abundance, and a miraculous life.

~~~~~~~~~~~~~~~~~~~~

Trish's story: Trish enrolled in Miracle Coaching shortly after receiving her degree in holistic medicine. Her intention for the program was to clear blocks so that she could create a thriving practice. She was a dedicated and motivated student and enjoyed each of the lessons. But during her program something happened that challenged her on many levels. She was contacted by her school and told that because of a technicality she would not be receiving her diploma. Trish was scared and angry and saw this as the end of her dream. Without her diploma she could not open her healing practice and work with clients. After years of study and hard work, she was devastated by this news.

During our sessions Trish had described some of her difficult child-hood experiences, which included having an authoritative mother whose interference and unreasonable demands on Trish's time and energy prevented her from doing what she wanted in her life. She saw this as one more way that an authority figure in her life was trying to block her success. While Trish saw her experiences with the school as impossible to overcome, I thought they were an excellent opportunity for her to use her authority to create her miracles.

We started with some affirming statements, that she deserved to receive her diploma, she had the authority to insist on it, and she would receive it. I reminded her that she had a choice, to give up and accept their decision, or to exert her authority over the situation and create the outcome she wanted. And that is what she did.

Despite her fears and doubts, Trish contacted the school and spoke to the administrator, insisting that they honor their commitment to her and give her the diploma. And they did, without arguing with her. This was a tremendous breakthrough for Trish, one that allowed her to overcome her belief that others had control over her life and enabled her to use her authority to create the outcome she wanted. She now saw herself as the authority in her life and knew that she would never again question who was in control of her reality.

Exercise: As you review your Miracle List today remember that you are the authority in your life, that you have the authority and the power to create your reality and that you (and only you) have any control over what happens in your life.

Do each of your miracles reflect your level of authority?

Have you asked for them with authority and conviction?

Do you need to be more authoritative in how you express your miracles on your Miracle List, using power phrases like "I have" and "I am"?

Is there someone in your life who interferes with your success? What do you do when they connect with you in this way?

Have they influenced how you ask or what you ask for, and what you think you will receive?

Do you ever think that you need someone's permission to do what you want to do?

If so, re-state your miracles so they reflect the authority that you have in your life.

If you have doubts about your ability to create miracles, remember that you are the authority in your life and the author of your life story. What kind of story do you want to create today?

Day 24 Don't Worry, Be Happy

Worry is the expression of our fear. We never worry about the things that are not important to us or that we are not uncertain about. If the Sun didn't rise tomorrow we would all be in trouble, but does anyone worry about the Sun not rising in the morning? When we worry about issues, situations or problems that we are experiencing, we relive our fear about them, over and over again. But worry has a far greater consequence, as it is a way we limit the flow of energy in our life and it keeps us in the energy of whatever we are worrying about. And as long as we continue to worry we will not be able to move beyond whatever it is we are worried about. Our worries keep us in the cycle of fear, failure, victim consciousness, and disappointment and they prevent us from creating miracles.

What we worry about shows us what we are afraid of. When we worry about our job, it is a sign to us that we have fear around it. When we worry about a relationship, the energy of that relationship is fear and is not unconditional love. When we are so uncertain about a situation that we must worry about it, it is a sign to us that we are out of the effortless flow of Universal energy. Worry is also a sign that we feel out of control. With worry we feel uncomfortable and disconnected, which means that we need to re-align our energy and consider an option to move in another direction. But we often interpret the worry to mean that we are doing something wrong, are not in control, or that by worrying we are preventing something even more unpleasant from happening.

That is not the case. When we worry we are living in the past, basing our future on what has already happened to us before. And when we worry about the future, our attention is not in the present moment. If we live in the present moment and know that everything always happens in perfection and with divine timing, and we have nothing to worry about. And when we are focused on manifesting miracles in our life, we have nothing to fear because we are using the power of our intention, trust, and faith to keep ourselves in the flow of the creation of our miracles.

For example, if one of your miracles was to find a new or different job, you may worry about losing your job. But that is what has to happen in order for the job change to occur. If your past experiences with changing jobs was difficult, you will worry that you may have to suffer and struggle to find a new job. Or if your current job situation is challenging, you may worry that you won't be able to find a new job with a more satisfactory work environment.

But when you are working with the miracle process, every transition can be effortless and happen at exactly the right time so that you step out of one job and directly into another. You can make that happen when you focus on creating miracles and do not worry about how the process will unfold.

Remember that one of the foundations of creating miracles is trust—you must trust in the process, in the Universe, and most importantly, in your own power and potential. When you are in complete trust and have faith in the process, there is no need to worry. All happens with divine timing in the best and most wonderful way possible.

So don't worry; be happy that you have found and connected to your power and stand in the place where you can create miracles and they will come to you effortlessly without the need to worry.

~~~~~~~~~~~~~~~~~~

Simon's story: Simon thought Miracle Coaching would help him control his fear which he admitted affected every aspect of his life. In fact, Simon knew that he worried too much and his high blood pressure proved it. As the owner of a growing and successful business, Simon worried constantly about revenues, customers, products, and keeping his investors happy. When he began the program he had just accepted a major financing package and while he was happy that his investors had enough confidence in his business to provide him with this funding, it also gave him many more things to worry about.

When I explained to Simon that he worried about everything because he feared losing control of his life, he found the source of his worrying. His parents had died when he was six years old and Simon spent his childhood living with various relatives, never knowing how long he would stay with one family before he was moved to another one. He felt he had no control over his life and worried about who would take care of him.

Simon remembered that worrying was a constant part of his young life, which carried over into adulthood. No matter how successful he was, there was always a fear that everything would fall apart and he would be homeless, helpless and unwanted, as he had been during his childhood.

With this realization came a breakthrough and a release of his worry and fear. Simon focused on the aspects of his life that he could control, those that would ensure his security, such as running his business and working with his customers. As he began to spend less time worrying he had more time and energy to focus on his business and his new fearless attitude enabled him to implement new and progressive plans that would help him meet his revenue goals and keep his investors happy. Simon also found that when he was not worrying he could enjoy his success and appreciate the life he had created for himself.

~~~~~~~~~~~~~~~~~

Exercise: With today's Miracle List review, write down any worries you have about your miracles.

Are you worried they won't happen?

Are you worried about possible changes they may create in your life and that you may lose control in some way?

Are you worried that your miracles won't happen effortlessly, or that you won't recognize them?

Are you worried about how others may react? Or that you may not know how to use your power in the best way?

Your worries are one way of expressing your fears. As they arise, resist the temptation to worry out of habit and instead, look at them to find their source and meaning in your life. As you do, you will learn to identify, name, work through, and release the fears that create what you worry about.

So be grateful they have presented themselves and remember that, in spite of your worries, you do have the power to create miracles and they will happen for you in the best way possible.

Day 25 Stop Trying

Are you 'trying' to change your life, lose weight, to find a better job, to get more money, to be happy, or to be successful?

Are you 'trying' to be happier, more spiritual, more connected, less judgmental, and to create miracles?

How many times do you say you are 'trying' to do things and you find that you never meet your goals?

Stop trying. Nothing changes when we 'try'. The Universe only recognizes what we are willing to do and be in the present moment. And if we tell the Universe that we are 'trying,' it will respond by giving us more opportunities to try.

When we say that we are trying, we are acknowledging our lack of abilities and failure and what we are really saying is that we hope, if all goes well, that we will somehow be successful at some point in the future. But trying is not the same thing as doing and when we are always trying, it's a sign that whatever we are trying to do isn't working and the energy isn't flowing very smoothly. 'Trying' gives our energy a focus but what we 'try' at is often a source of frustration. What have you tried to do in the past and found yourself going around in circles? Think of the difference in energy between saying 'I am trying' and 'I will'.

What is the more intentional statement? Do you intend to try or do you intend to do?

Stop here for a moment and look at your Miracle List. Have you written 'I intend to try' or used the word 'try' in any of them? When you created your Miracle List, you were asked to write them in positive, active language. How do you feel about them if you begin each one with some aspect of trying? They don't feel as positive, or as possible, do they?

We use the word 'trying' to describe situations or events where we are working towards some goal but have not yet reached it. We also use the word 'trying' to acknowledge that we have been working hard at something but just can't seem to make it happen. Or we use the word 'trying' to convince ourselves that we can do something when we secretly doubt that we can. When we say that we are trying, we are reminding ourselves that we do not think we can succeed at what we are doing.

If you have read the book *The Difference Between a Victim and a Victor is I AM* you know that I suggest that we take the word 'trying' out of our vocabulary, because it has victim energy and only serves to remind us that whatever we are 'trying' at is not working out for us.

Instead, we should focus on doing, being, and having. These are active words that exist in the present moment. When we are doing what we love, being our best self, having everything that we want, we acknowledge that we are in control of our life. When we 'try' we are putting forth effort but are unsure of the outcome.

One of the principles of miracle creation is to know, without doubt, that what we are creating is already part of our reality. We do not have to 'try' for it is already happening, the energy is in motion, and the miracle is on its way. It will come to us at the right time, in the most perfect way and will be wonderful beyond what we can imagine.

But if we put ourselves in the 'trying' mentality, our miracles will wait to manifest until we can stop trying, meaning that we are putting our energy towards actions and intentions that are not flowing effortlessly, another example of our 'no pain, no gain' mentality. When we are willing to stop trying, we allow ourselves to connect with people and situations that are so well aligned with our energy and intention, that everything flows smoothly to us and we don't have to try because it all manifests without any challenges. If we have to use the word 'try' or 'trying' to convince ourselves that we are making an effort, even if nothing is working out, then we need to put our energy towards something else.

~~~~~~~~~~~~~~~~~~

Jeff's story: Jeff saw Miracle Coaching as his last option to gain control over his life. He was struggling in every area, working at a job he disliked, his marriage was in trouble, his aging parents' health was failing, and he was considering whether he should move them closer to his home or move closer to theirs. He was under so much stress and pressure that he was in a constant state of worry and was not sleeping well. In Jeff's words, he had spent his life 'trying to do the right thing' for everyone and never felt that he succeeded.

All of the miracles on Jeff's Miracle List used the world 'trying', as in ' trying to get ahead in my job', 'trying to help my parents,' 'trying to create a stable marriage.' As we discussed them he mentioned that he had been trying to accomplish these things for many years and had been frustrated by his inability to succeed in creating what he wanted in his life. He felt burdened by his many obligations and they stood in the way of his progress. So we focused on the obligations because they represented the blocks in his life. As Jeff made a list of his obligations, including the people and situations they represented, he had his break-through when he said 'It looks like I have been trying to make everyone happy but me.'

Now Jeff had a choice to make, to continue to try to please others or to focus his energies on his own accomplishments. In some cases there were synergies but he also had to decide what he was willing to let go of in order to free up some of his time and energy to work on his own life.

I had him re-phrase each miracle on his Miracle List and replace the world 'trying' with the phrases 'I have', 'I am' or 'I will'. About half of the miracles on his list were removed when he realized that most of what he was trying to do he really did not want to do at all, or they represented things he was trying to do for other people, in violation of their free will.

Jeff accepted that each person was in control of their joy and happiness and that no matter how hard he tried, he had no control over anyone's life choices. That helped him feel better about his decision to stop 'trying' to make everyone else happy and begin to choose what he wanted for his life. And when he stopped taking responsibility for everyone's happiness, he allowed others to step in and offer suggestions for his parents' care that gave him the support he needed. This removed some of the pressure from his life so he was able to focus on the things he 'wanted' to do, such as staying in his own home, finding a new job, and improving his marriage.

~~~~~~~~~~~~~~~~~~~~

Exercise: Do you speak of your miracles in terms of what you are 'trying' to do? Stop trying. Use the words, be, do, and have to describe your miracles, for the energy to create them is set in motion as soon as you ask. Remind yourself to replace the word 'trying' with other words that imply action accomplishment and success, which is much more powerful and focuses on doing, not trying.

Look at what you are 'trying' to do in your life and if something is not working, perhaps it is a sign to you that it is not right for you and it needs to be released so you can focus your energy in other directions.

As you read your Miracle List every day, remember that you are creating miracles, you have what you want, you are successful, and you are doing exactly the right thing at the right time to allow your miracles to flow effortlessly to you.

Jennifer Hoffman

Day 26 Practice Makes Perfect

We learn to use our power through practice, just as we learn anything new by practicing it on a regular basis. If you want to learn to play a musical instrument, for example, you must practice every day until you can master it. And so it is with creating miracles. This is not a power that you must save for the important things in your life, it is not something that you have a limited amount of, or are limited in your ability to use.

Creating miracles is an expression of your spiritual power, it is you in action, a testament to the acknowledgement and acceptance of your divinity and Source connection. When you call forth the energy of miracles to create your life, every day, you acknowledge your own Source power, become more familiar and comfortable with the process, and it becomes a process of deliberate, intentional, and conscious creation that you use in your life, in the same way that you breathe air to stay alive.

Because we can think that miracles are reserved for major or important life needs, we may be tempted to use our ability to create miracles until we really need them. That is not necessary and we can use our miracle ability meet every daily need. Creating miracles is how we channel and express our universal energy connection and when we manage our energy in this way, we are always in conscious control of where we are placing our energetic resources.

For this reason, we cannot judge the value or importance of our miracles. Everything is equal in the eyes of the Universe and it will grant us whatever we ask for. So while we may classify miracles as being big or small, important or unimportant, whether we ask for five miracles or five thousand miracles, each one is important in the eyes of the Universe and is granted equal attention, and then created at the perfect time.

Practicing miracles is easy, we simply ask for what we want, whenever we want it. We can ask for anything, including a parking space when we need to park the car close to the door because it's cold, rainy or we don't feel like walking very far. Know that the parking spot will appear at the right moment and then trust that it will happen. Using our ability to create miracles every day, every time we need something, brings us many benefits and it helps us consciously work with the Law of Attraction. It makes us more familiar with how energy works and how to use it, and it builds our faith and trust in the process. Sometimes it's easier to manifest small miracles, such as a glass of water or a seat on the subway, than larger ones, like a new house, a job, or a relationship simply because we believe that the smaller, 'less important' miracles are easier to manifest.

That is not how the Universe works, but we need to build our faith and confidence so that we can effortlessly manifest what we think are larger or more important miracles, such as a new house or job, a desired vacation, like a trip to France, or a new relationship.

To practice creating miracles, simply ask for what you want, whenever you want it. Remember to use your intention and remove any fears you have that they won't happen. And then activate your belief and intention and pay attention to what happens next. Miracles can come to us in unexpected ways and we need to ensure that we are aware of what is going on around us (by being in the present moment) so that we don't miss the signs that our miracles have arrived.

Practice your miracle creation every day, asking for whatever you want in your life and you will manifest an effortless flow of miracles. When you ask for miracles you have the Universe's undivided attention, as it doesn't have more important things to do than help you with your miracles. As you focus on your Miracle List, remind yourself that your miracles are on their way to you, and you can use this process to fulfill every need in your life.

Practice makes perfect and the more you practice your miracle creation abilities, the more you perfect your skills, become comfortable with the process, and are able to create miracles every day and in every situation.

~~~~~~~~~~~~~~~~~~~

Peggy's story: Peggy wanted to learn how to create miracles in her life and she was very eager to start Miracle Coaching. Her biggest challenge was creating her Miracle List because she felt that she already had everything she needed and since there were people in the world who needed miracles more than she did, she felt guilty about asking for more. As we talked about what miracles were, a shift in personal consciousness and a movement of energy, and how they were available to everyone, even those who did not seem to ask for them, Peggy realized that there were miracles that she did want. She wanted to be more confident, release her fears and anxiety, to have others acknowledge her needs and to take a vacation at the beach.

By creating her Miracle List to reflect aspects of herself that she wanted to transform, she also realized how she had been limiting her life, and spending her time and energy feeling guilty about her successes, and feeling sorry for other people. Focusing on her miracles allowed her to acknowledge that she had always put others' needs before hers, thinking that she was not important. It was not easy to convince her that she could use her miracle powers for everyday needs, such as finding a parking place when she went to the shopping mall. But she was willing to practice and learned to focus her intention and was soon able to create miracles effortlessly.

Peggy's breakthrough was an amazing journey into knowing that she could create miracles and use this energy in her life, and deserved to have what she wanted, even if she was aware that other people were struggling. She realized that her miracles did not belong to someone else and that there were enough miracles for everyone.

Peggy did learn to value herself and her power and to expand her thinking about what was possible for her. And she even did something she had always wanted to do, manifest a guilt-free vacation at the beach, which was one of the miracles on her list.

~~~~~~~~~~~~~~~~~~~

Exercise: As you review your Miracle List, do you think that some miracles are more important than others?

Do you think that the smaller or less important miracles have a better chance of occurring than the larger ones?

Are you focusing more on the ones you think will manifest for you, instead of the ones you really want?

Are you reluctant to ask for miracles because you think there are so many people in the world with greater or more important needs than yours?

Remember that everything is equal in the Universe, so nothing is less than or greater than anything else. Each of your miracles is as important as any other miracle and receives the same consideration, attention, and level of fulfillment as the miracles that everyone else in the world is asking for. And everyone has the power to create miracles, it is an ability that is part of our personal power because we are energetic beings and moving energy is an ability that everyone has.

Write any revisions of miracles you wrote on your Miracle List and re-order them, in case you have put the ones you think are possible first, rather than the ones you want. You can add new miracles to replace those that have already occurred.

Remember to congratulate yourself for having created your miracles too, acknowledging yourself for what you create is part of your active miracle process.

Day 27 Patience and Trust

Patience is part of the experience of miracle manifestation because we usually judge the success of our miracles by how long they take to manifest. With miracles we are in the realm of divine timing, which is multi-dimensional, simultaneous, and does not depend on the passage of hours, days, weeks, and months. Miracles are a flow of timing, which is an energetic perspective that involves working on an energetic level and within a different time perspective. Human timing is linear, where one thing follows another and the first thing must be completed before the second can begin. With divine timing everything happens simultaneously and at the best and most perfect moment.

With human timing we have 'God, please help me' moments, when we believe change and results are absolutely and immediately necessary. Then we panic when things don't manifest as quickly as we think they should because we are in fear. We cannot see that all of our prayers are in the process of being answered because within our human concept of time, we that miracle manifestation depends on time. And it doesn't, it is a process of energy flow that takes into account our energetic vibrations and frequency, what we have asked for, how aligned we are with it, and how to create the miracle in manner that answers our conscious and unconscious needs, and gives us what we asked for, and more if that is possible.

From a spiritual and energetic perspective, all solutions to our miracles are being processed at the same time, including aligning all possible sources of manifestation, so the right and best result, from the most perfect source, is created for us. Miracles come to us with divine timing, not within our own, human timing.

When we step out of our human timing's need to see immediate or necessary results we are in touch with our spiritual power and then time and timing, need, desperation and our life emergencies become irrelevant. From this perspective we don't have to worry about anything because we know that everything is being handled effortlessly, no matter how long that process appears to take. And remember that miracles are a shift in energy that mirrors our energy. If they aren't manifesting quickly, we need to look within ourselves to find out where the block is. We are aware that there is a flow to everything and a divine order in our life. Instant gratification is not promised to us when we work with miracles but perfect results are. Patience is how we show that we trust in the divine perfection of the process.

In our impatience, which is fueled by our fear and worry, we are tempted to work harder, pray more and ask for more miracles, when the delays are hints to slow down, breathe, renew our faith and trust, and remember that life unfolds in responds to a flow of energy. When we are desperate for something to happen to remove the chaos, drama, and pain, we are in the throes of fear and believe that every effort we make should be towards resolving or fixing our situation. Yet the fear is blocking the miracles and we must first address and resolve our fear to get the energy moving.

Sometimes we believe there is a 'fast track' to miracles and to creating the life of our dreams. But this ignores the journey and its many blessings.

As we try to speed through the process it appears to slow down as we are asked to become the observer and step out of the frenzy of emotions into the calm of patience. As the observer we can view our pain and chaos as the result of choices we made in our journey of growth and healing, take responsibility and remember the lessons we wanted to learn from them. But the focus on physical, mental or emotional pain and chaos and our rush to eliminate them limits our awareness of any progress that is occurring in other areas of our life.

As the observer we can practice detachment in the face of our pain and chaos and ask questions such as:

How did I create this?

Is this a pattern in my life?

Did I choose this consciously or unconsciously?

Was I using my power in this situation or did I give it to someone else?

The Universe sometimes appears to ignore us and our pleas for help when we are in our greatest time of need. But it is infinitely patient and waits for us to remember that we are powerful, in control, that our reality is our creation and we are the ones who have the authority and power to change it. When we have stepped out of our fear that things won't happen on time or at the right time, and can be patient with the process, allowing divine timing to unfold, we create space for the Universe to help us to move the energy and create miracles from our enlightened position of power, trust, control, and faith.

Being patient is how we maintain this control and display our trust in the miracle process.

We learn patience through trial and error and after many attempts to rush through our lessons and fix what we believe is broken we realize that the purpose of any spiritual journey is not the destination, as the blessings lie in the journey itself. There is purpose and meaning in each step we take, and each choice contains answers to our questions of why we are here, what is our purpose, and how we can achieve lasting joy and peace.

The Universe is not trying to deny us what we want, it is merely ensuring that we are aware of all of the conditions and circumstances that surround our situation and rediscover our inner power. By appearing to delay the process, it is helping us see how we have created it so we don't do it again. This also helps us align with the new levels of energy that will allow us to create different options and new potentials. Within the delay we have time to reflect on whether we have learned everything we need from this moment and strategize to transform our beliefs and thinking to create a different reality. Anything that appears to be a delay also helps us understand the sequence of events that led to the situation we are in so we fully understand how we use our power in creating our reality. We are aware of this through our willingness to be patient, to listen to our guidance, to calm the voice of our fears and be open to the wisdom and knowledge that we can only learn through patience.

The Universe always works with us when we create miracles, as long as we are aware that divine timing is always working in our favor and on our behalf, are patient and have faith that our miracles come to us in the best, most wonderful, and perfect way possible.

~~~~~~~~~~~~~~~~~~~~~~

Anne's story: Anne enrolled in Miracle Coaching to help her cope with her divorce process, which had lasted over two years and was still not finished. She was tired of the court dates, lawyers, fights, and arguments and wanted to create a miracle that would end it. And her Miracle List contained only two miracles, that her divorce end soon and that she had the resources to support herself and her children.

As our sessions progressed it was clear that Anne's divorce was not really about ending her marriage, it was a journey in understanding her power and her responsibility in her life. She had relinquished her power to her husband during her marriage and the lengthy divorce process was allowing her to regain it. While she just wanted it to be over so she could move on with her life, she had not gone through the process of understanding why she had created this situation in her life and the delayed divorce was helping her do that.

She was angry with her husband's attitude but angrier with herself for all of the many ways she had allowed him to control her life during their marriage. It became clear, as we worked through these issues, that until she stopped being angry, the divorce would continue to drag on.

Learning detachment and how to control her energy and her emotions were part of her lessons in this life experience.

Although Anne wanted her divorce to be over, she was willing to be patient with the process and to use the time to go within to gain perspective on the path she had chosen, to see how she had been repeating this cycle, which involved victim consciousness, at other times in her life and consider the other options she had for her future. She realized that without her willingness to understand this process she could miss its lessons, and repeat them in her next relationship. Her divorce could even be delayed indefinitely. She understood that the principle of divine timing, which she thought was her enemy, was actually helping her to reconnect with her power and release her victim beliefs so she could learn to choose a more balanced, powerful life once it was finished.

Exercise: As you review your Miracle List today consider where your patience has been rewarded or where you are becoming impatient because your miracles have not yet manifested.

How does this make you feel? Are you ready to quit or can you see how the delay is helping you in other areas of your life?

Write down how you feel about each miracle that has not yet manifested and one or two things you are learning from waiting for them to appear in your life.

Relax, have patience and become the observer. The delays you are experiencing are opportunities to express gratitude for what you have, remember who is powerful in your life, and affirm your faith and trust.

Miracles are sometimes a lesson in patience and when we understand and accept the principle of divine timing, we acknowledge that everything that we need comes to us at exactly the right time and in the right way.

Jennifer Hoffman

Day 28 Believe In Yourself

Your Miracle List represents your willingness to acknowledge your potential and the abundance that is available to you. Every miracle we ask for reflects our belief in our power and abilities. With this belief you can move mountains, which means removing all obstacles to creating an effortless, miraculous life. All it requires is that you believe in yourself.

What we want from others is to be validated and loved. And they do give us those things, but in a way that reflects their ability to love and their beliefs about themselves, their self worth, their value, and how much they deserve to receive and have love. When someone tells you 'I don't think you can do that', what they are actually saying is because they don't believe that it is something they are capable of doing or being, so they don't think you can either.

Take a moment to remember the last time you shared a dream or goal with someone who told you that you could not do that. How did you feel? Did you feel invalidated and unloved? Was their disapproval enough to make you abandon your dream?

Can you consider that the person you asked was actually mirroring your own self doubt back to you so you could be aware of it and move forward anyway?

Or that they were showing you their own doubts and fears?

Did their disapproval cause you to affirm your belief in yourself or make you think that perhaps you weren't as capable as you thought you were?

Each one of us looks to others to fill our need for love, respect, and value. And what we receive mirrors our own beliefs about ourselves because that is what we are attracting. Instead of feeling discouraged when others don't meet our needs by responding to us in a negative way, we should appreciate the important lesson they are giving us about where we need to increase our self-love and learn to believe in ourselves.

Because we look to those we respect and value to mirror the best in us we accept their opinions of who we are as our truth. And we allow their opinions to become the measure of our belief in ourselves and our abilities. How many of your opinions about yourself are yours and which ones reflect those of others that you have accepted as your own truth?

What about your negative opinions of yourself, the ones that tell you 'aren't good enough' or 'will never succeed'? A simple statement that someone made to us, at any time in our life, that we interpret as meaning that we cannot be successful, create what we want, or meet a goal, will create self-doubt that affects every area of our life. Then we allow the opinions of others to become the truth of our being and we limit ourselves and our lives to the expression of that truth.

Each of us begins life with limitless potential and over time our belief in that potential is slowly eroded by years of self doubt, criticism, and judgment. The Universe knows that we are perfect and complete just as we are. When we believe in ourselves we are remembering who we are and affirming our own perfection. Your Miracle List affirms your ability to believe in yourself and when you do, a life of miraculous possibilities is available to you.

~~~~~~~~~~~~~~~~~~~~

Amy's story: Amy is one of the few Miracle Coaching students who was unhappy with the results of her program, although she did create some of her miracles. Since she was unable to manifest what she considered to be the most important miracle on her list, to find a job and move out her of father's home, she thought she had not successfully completed the program.

Amy had moved in with her father after an unexpected and distressing job layoff. She loved her job and was very sad that she had lost it. After six months she still had not looked for another job and was very frustrated with the situation. She was angry with her former employer and did not understand why they had let her go because she was a good employee and performed well at her job. Her relationship with her father was not a happy one either and the emotional distance between them made living there uncomfortable for Amy. She remembered him as being critical, cold and unsupportive so it was particularly hard to be with him at a time when she really needed someone to give her positive encouragement to help her through this situation.

The layoff had caused her to doubt herself and her abilities and she was afraid to become attached to a company in case another layoff happened. She acknowledged that she had taken the layoff personally and knew that others had lost their jobs too. But she could not overcome her fears of another layoff, so although she felt stuck and was unhappy, she did not look for another job. Amy said that taking care of her father took a lot of her time but she had lost her confidence and it was easier for her to stay at home and convince herself that she was too busy caring for him to look for a new job.

Amy admitted that unless her father put pressure on her to leave the house she would probably stay there even though she felt that she was not progressing in her life. And by become his caretaker, she was unconsciously receiving the attention she had always wanted from him. It was hard for her to fully admit that she was victimizing herself to get her father to value her, but it was true. And until Amy made the commitment to believe in herself and trust that she would find the right job— and if that job ended she would find another one, she would stay where she was.

There were other miracles on her list that Amy was able to create but because she was attached to this one, she did not think they were as important. Because she was not willing to trust in the Universe and believe in herself, she was unable to move forward and was stuck in a cycle of unhappiness and self doubt that would continue until she was willing to release it.

Exercise: As you review your Miracle List today can you remember any opinions or comments others made to you that created doubt about your abilities or limited your belief in yourself?

Is there someone whose approval and validation you want to have so much that you are willing to victimize yourself to receive it?

For each miracle on your list write down a limiting belief about it.

Then write another expansive belief about it.

If you can, try to remember where and when that limiting belief started, whether it was from a conversation, a judgment, criticism, or a belief you developed from an experience you had.

Remember that when you believe in yourself you are mirroring the Universe's belief in you.

You can create a new opinion about yourself that affirms your worthiness, value and your ability to create miracles.

Do it today so you can transform your negative opinions into positive ones and believe in yourself.

Day 29 Be, Do, Act

Our state of being, who we believe and think we are, is mirrored back to us in every aspect of our life. We see examples of our state of being in our friends, our job, where we live, and who and what we attract into our lives. As we know from the Law of Attraction, if we want to change what we attract, we must start with ourselves.

This is also true with miracle manifestation. If you believe that you will be happier and more fulfilled when you receive your miracles the best time to start being that happy, fulfilled person is now. That is what will raise your vibrations and attract what you want to you. And it's hard to convince yourself that you deserve your miracles when you are sad and unhappy.

No matter how close or far you are from the results, your state of being will determine how quickly or slowly that process occurs. Sometimes you must convince yourself that this is true long before you see the physical results in your life, especially when you have old beliefs to overcome. Before anything can materialize in your life you have to create the energy for it.

Can you be the person you want to be when your miracles manifest right now, even if you are scared, impatient, and confused?

Try imagining what you will feel like when your miracles manifest. Hold that feeling until you can remember it in vivid detail. Now each time you feel doubtful or afraid, recall that feeling. This is 'being' your miracles, connecting with the state of being that your miracles create within you. You do not have to wait for your miracles manifest to be in their energy. In fact, they will manifest much more quickly if you can be in their energy now. Remember that miracles they are created as soon as you ask for them. Start today, to be the confident, joyful, fulfilled person you think you will be when your miracles appear in your life. This also activates the Law of Attraction and speeds the process of your miracle manifestation because you are working with the energy flow and not against it.

We are reminded that we are human beings, not human doings and yet so much of our daily life is spent doing things. But what are we really doing? Are we just busy 'trying' so we feel like we're doing something, or is there a purpose to what we do? Is it fulfilling any current need or desire in our life or are we just filling our time with busy work while we wait for our real life, the one we will enjoy, to begin?

If we take a moment to stop and review what we do with our time, we will see that much of it is spent in unfocused busy work. Can we focus our state of doing on the miracles we want to create, spending a part of each day in doing the things that will help them manifest?

Every new beginning has a learning curve, that period of time where we are disoriented and confused until we can acquire and master new life skills. And we have to learn these skills 'on the job', acting 'as if' we knew what we were doing until we move beyond the learning curve. This may mean trying different options before we find the ones that work for us. And this is also true of the miracle process. We can make today, this moment, the starting point where we will be happy, feel confident, and bask in the assurance that our miracles are in the process of manifesting.

Whether our miracles occur in the next five minutes or in five months, we can act as if they have already occurred because they have in spirit, we are simply giving the mind time to catch up with the new possibilities we have created for our lives. We can be as positive, confident and happy now as we will be when they are in front of us. Remember that miracles begin when we ask for them and we can act as if our miracles have already happened because in the eyes of the Universe, they already have.

The Universe includes our energetic vibration in the miracle process and manifests from our lowest vibration, so when we are being, doing and acting our miracles we are creating the vibrations that will match and manifest them.

~~~~~~~~~~~~~~~~~

Ashley's story: Ashley enrolled in Miracle Coaching because she wanted to create a new career but was not sure what she wanted to do. She hoped the program would give her clarity about her new career path. Her Miracle List was focused on gaining clarity about her path, the hope that she would be happier in her new career, and that she would find the fulfillment in life that she was looking for.

At the time, Ashley worked as an administrative assistant but was frustrated by the lack of appreciation her employer showed for her skills and hard work. She wanted to express her true potential and be recognized for it.

Our first focus was to uncover what Ashley was passionate about, the one thing that she wished she could do. After some thought, Ashley quietly said that she had always wanted to be a lawyer but followed the comment with 'I don't think I am smart enough to go to law school and I probably can't afford it anyway.' Ashley had informally studied law and followed big legal cases. Several of her friends had told her that she should go to law school but she never followed up on their suggestion. Some of Ashley's homework assignments included purchasing a study guide for the LSAT, to visit an admissions counselor at her local law school and learn what was required to become a law student, things Ashley had never considered doing before.

While she was intimidated by the homework assignment, she did it anyway and was surprised to learn that she would be able to enroll in the school if she passed the LSAT, could get financial aid to pay for law school, and that there were special scholarship programs at this university for women students seeking a career change. Now all she had to make the decision to go because the blocks she thought existed were not there any longer.

Ashley was very excited that her secret desire was on the threshold of becoming a reality and with this new information she could be more confident of her chances of success. I reminded her that the 'be, do, act' principle of miracles meant that we have to be willing to listen to the guidance that is provided to us, which can come from the suggestions we hear from others, to give us direction. Unless we are willing to explore opportunities and do our homework, our dreams can remain unfulfilled. We must be willing to take action and to be in the energy of our miracles, in spite of our fears, for them to manifest.

And that includes informing ourselves of the possibilities that exist and taking the leap of faith that will help us find our wings.

~~~~~~~~~~~~~~~~~~

Exercise: As you review your Miracle List today focus on the 'be, do, act' that is part of the process.

What do you have to be to help your miracles manifest?

Do you have to be more confident, trusting, forceful or more aware of where your energy is going?

Who and what you are being helps set the energy, intention and focus for your miracles. They reflect what you have always wanted to be and you do not have to wait for them to manifest to start 'being' your miracles.

What are you doing to support your miracles? You are a co-creator with the Universe and what you do directs the energy so that it is constantly flowing towards your miracles and that includes doing whatever is necessary to put yourself in their energetic vibration.

What can you do to put yourself in the state of acting 'as if' you already had your miracles?

Can you see them occurring in the present moment instead of at some point in the future?

Can you act like the positive, confident, happy person you believe you will be when your miracles manifest?

Act 'as if' your miracles have already happened and you will help bring them into your life.

For each of your miracles, write what 'be, do, act' means for them. Then start doing it today. This helps set the energy for your miracles and shows the Universe that you are a confident and willing co-creator, with total and absolute trust and faith in the process.

Day 30 Recognizing Your Miracles

If our miracles can come to us in different and unusual ways, how do we know that they have happened? How do we know that we have manifested what we want in our lives if it doesn't always look like what we were expecting to receive? Recognizing the miracles that have manifested is challenged by our expectations and judgments of them.

Our expectations may cause us to overlook our miracles because the results may not be what we thought would happen.

Our judgments may cause us to limit how our miracles can manifest because we constrict the energy flow by creating such narrow boundaries that the Universe cannot fulfill them to the full extent possible. And to recognize them, we must be paying attention and living in the present moment.

In the miracle story that I shared with you at the beginning of this book, I had no expectations about how I would go to France that summer. I simply wanted to go very badly. And the way I received the trip, going as an interpreter on a tour, was a complete surprise. I didn't even know that this was possible. Had I expected to receive the money for the trip and ignored the interpreter offer, I would have missed the miracle entirely. And the way I received the message, in an email from someone I had not heard from in a long time, should be noted too. I almost didn't read that email and if I had not read it and replied to it, I might have missed the fulfillment of my miracle.

Remember that miracles are not about creating money to pay for things, they are simply about getting what we want. How that comes to us is up to the Universe and it will create amazing and unexpected outcomes that deliver what we want, sometimes in ways we would never have considered possible. The Universe has promised that it will always fulfill our desires and it always keeps its promises.

Letting go of our expectations and judgments provides the Universe with a clear path to bring our miracles to us. Recognizing them then becomes easy because we simply see the miracle and are not concerned with the details. Our perspective on the possible outcomes for our miracles is so small, compared to that of the Universe, that when we place expectations or have judgments as to how our miracles will manifest, we limit the Universe's ability to create the best possible path and outcome for them.

Miracles can arrive in steps or stages and may not present themselves in a logical order. Our willingness to consider every opportunity allows us to refrain from judging anything that manifests and be open to considering what may at first appear to be a mistake. Sometimes we have to go through a first door, to try a first opportunity, and our miracle is at the next door or within the next opportunity.

And we can also receive options that allow us to say 'no' to what is not quite right for us and to allow something else to materialize. We never have to settle for what does not meet our needs and by learning to say 'no' we affirm our trust that something more suitable is available.

You have dedicated the past 30 days to creating miracles. Were you able to manifest any of the miracles you wrote on your Miracle List? You may have seen some of your miracles manifest and others may have become less important. Perhaps you re-wrote your entire Miracle List because you decided to ask for other things. This is part of the process. Once you are able to connect with your power to create miracles your perspective on your life and the possibilities that are available to you expands exponentially.

Are there some miracles on your list that have not yet appeared in your life? Are you ready to give up on them out of frustration or disappointment? What you do now is important and now is not the time to give up although you may be tempted to. This may be a pattern in your life, where you lose hope and give up before you allow things to fully manifest.

Be patient, even though it may be difficult when you are facing your fears. The delay may be an opportunity for you to look at the beliefs and fears you have around the changes you wish to make. Instead of using the delay to feel hopeless and helpless, ask yourself if you need to re-write some of your miracles or are somehow blocking their manifestation. The delay is an opportunity to be patient and show your trust in the process, as well as learning about your fears and how you use your energy. Sometimes we need to release our initial Miracle List and create something entirely different.

We recognize our miracles by simply being aware that we always receive what we ask for and then pay attention to what manifests. And that happens when we are in the present moment, without any expectations of how the outcome can or will happen. Our miracles can arrive in many ways—through another person, divine intervention, a strange twist of fate, a chance meeting, hearing or seeing something in passing—the list of possibilities is endless. That is why it is important for us to simply trust that because we asked, and it is done. That's step one. Step two is to be in receiving mode, which means we aren't asking and looking around the corner for the result. We're believing, with trust and faith, that our miracles are on their way to us and all we have to do is receive (and of course, take action when we are guided to). And then remember that the Universe will use many different ways to help us manifest our miracles and we simply have to pay attention so we don't miss the clues or the manifestation of our miracles.

Marie's story: Marie had been on a spiritual path for many years and had taken numerous classes and seminars. She wanted to do the Miracle Coaching program because she was stuck, unable to move forward in her life. There were things she wanted to do but she got to a certain point in the process and then nothing happened. Her Miracle List showed her frustration as she mentioned that she was asking for these miracles 'again'.

During our first session we discussed what Maria had been doing to manifest her miracles, the actions she had taken and how she was using her energy to focus on them. With a busy life and full schedule, Maria did not have much time to spend on herself but she said that she tried to spend some time every day on her miracles. We discussed what had been happening and then it was clear—her miracles had been manifesting but she was not following through and completing the process.

One of her miracles was to manifest a new job and Maria was frustrated that had not yet happened. When I told her that sometimes miracles happened through others, she thought of a friend's recent lunch invitation that she had been too busy to accept. Her friend had mentioned meeting someone who worked in the industry Maria was interested in. I asked Maria if perhaps this person could be helpful in helping her find a job and that was the reason for the invitation. Then Maria thought of several other situations that could have been a first step towards her miracles but she thought that her miracles would come in a certain way and was not looking beyond her expectations.

Although Maria trusted in the process, she was overlooking possibilities to connect to her miracles because she was not taking advantage of all of the opportunities that were being presented to her. She made a commitment to pay attention to every situation that crossed her path, accept invitations to meet others and to remember that she had stepped into the flow of miracles so everything in her life was working to bring them to her.

~~~~~~~~~~~~~~~~~~~~

Exercise: Review your Miracle List today and congratulate yourself for any miracles you have already created. If there are a few you're still waiting for, are you becoming impatient? Are you ready to give up on them? This may be a critical moment for you and may be part of your pattern of giving up just before the end is near.

Do you have any judgments or expectations about how the miracles on your list will come to you? Be open to all possibilities, without judging them. For each miracle on your list, write down as many ways that it could happen, getting as creative as possible. Don't forget to include that it could be a gift or be given to you because that is always a possibility.

Sometimes a miracle appears in steps or stages. Other people are sometimes the 'angels' that deliver our miracles to us.

Has something appeared that does not quite meet your needs? Don't be afraid to say 'no' and wait for something else. Simply trust that because you asked your miracles will, they must, come to you. And they will, with divine timing and in ways you may not expect.

And if all of your miracles have manifested, good for you. Celebrate your victory and create another Miracle List. This is how you can create your life and it is the way you will ensure that you are always in the flow of effortless, miraculous living.

You Create Your Good

You create everything in your life, including all of the good and wonderful things that bring you joy, and you are the only one who can. No one can make anything happen for you. If you look for a rescuer or someone to make your life better you will find yourself going from one situation to another, from one person to another, without finding the happiness you want. The good you want to create in your life starts with you. Others can participate in it but you have to set the intention and energy for it to happen.

When you wait for your good to come from others you are giving them the power to create your life and they will create according to their desired good, using their energies, abilities, and beliefs. Can someone else know or understand what is best or right for you? Sometimes you do this consciously, trusting that someone who has created something in their life that you want in yours has more power than you do or has greater abilities. Sometimes you do this unconsciously, believing that you are not worthy or deserving of the things you want in your life, or incapable of creating them.

How do you create your good? Your miracle list is one way because it reflects what you really want, the desires of your heart. We do not have random desires; everything we want is something that is available to us when we can connect with it. When you created your Miracle List you brought those things forward so you could manifest them. This is the good that you want in your life.

Because your miracles reflect the desires of your heart they are uniquely yours and have meaning for you alone. That is why you cannot create miracles on behalf of someone else and they cannot create them for you. You are the only one who knows and understands the good you want in your life, and why. See your Miracle List as a way of creating good in your life and know that this is the best use of your power, to create the life of your dreams.

Do you believe that you need other people to help you with this process? Is there a miracle on your list that you believe requires the participation of someone else? Are you worrying about whether that person will show up, will be the right person, or will be capable? Can you believe that you may be that person and that whatever is needed to manifest that miracle will show up at the right place and time?

Remember that you set the creative energy in your life and others respond to your beliefs about your power. You must set the energy for the joy and abundance in your life. No one can do that for you. You are the most powerful person in your life and you create your own good. See your list of miracles as a step towards creating your good and then you will attract the situations and people that will participate in the process with you. The Universe works with you, not for you. It provides guidance and assistance but it will never tell you what to do, or act outside of the boundaries of your own free will.

You have created miracles in your life in the last 30 days and I urge you to continue. When you receive all of the miracles on one list, create another one. Teach this skill to your children—give them the gift of knowing how to use their miracle power to create an abundant, fulfilling, and miraculous life.

Review your Miracle List daily, to remind yourself that you are responsible for creating your own good, all of the happiness, joy, peace, and love you want in your life comes from you, from the energy and intentions that you set for it.

For each miracle you create, write down the 'good' that it represents for you. This could be joy, security, stability, transformation or peace, as examples. Then keep the energy flowing by being, doing and acting as if you already had your miracles because you do, they're out in your field of potential, waiting for you to connect with them and bring them to earth, to become part of your reality.

Jennifer Hoffman

Creating Miracles for the World

We live in miraculous times but when we look at what is going on in the world it doesn't seem like things are getting any better than they have ever been. If anything, the world's problems seem to be getting worse instead of better. Why aren't we seeing more results, since so many people are choosing a different way of life, changing their perspective, and reconnecting with their spiritual nature? When we look at the world with human timing, things seem to be moving very slowly, if at all. But from the perspective of divine timing, many changes are occurring simultaneously, even if the results are not apparent to us. These are truly wonderful and miraculous times for us all but that does not mean that there will be an instantaneous release from all of our problems.

We are becoming more aware of our connection to each other, our role in the human family, our connection to Source and as we create miracles in our own lives and release our fear, doubt and confusion, we make the choice of miraculous living a possibility for everyone. The path of miracles is a journey from fear to unconditional love and each of us contributes to that process when we set an intention to live a miraculous life.

As we embrace our spiritual power and learn to create miracles each of us contributes to the spiritual growth of humanity and is able to

233

help raise the vibrations of many other people in the world. Our spiritual growth, acceptance of our spiritual nature and reclaiming our spiritual power raises our own vibrations and that, in turn, creates openings to allow everyone to raise their own vibrations.

When enough people are able to do this, we create a resonance in the world that all of humanity can join. And that will begin the process of creating miracles for the world.

As you review your list of miracles, you may think that you are asking for too much, being selfish, or meeting your needs at the expense of others. You may think it is self indulgent to ask for a new outfit, a new car, house, or a washer and dryer when there are so many people in the world who are sick, hungry, and poor. But each person has the ability to create miracles, and we are each part of a greater whole that can call upon Source, God or the Universe. When we ask for ourselves, we also ask on behalf of everyone else.

No, everyone in the world doesn't want a new outfit or a car but when each one of us assumes our mantle of power and realizes that we can create the details of our lives through setting intention and moving energy, we become victors and leave our victim consciousness behind. It is our willingness to accept, work with and be guided by this powerful connection that enables us to create miracles and it will enable us to change the energy of the world.

And it is our ability to know that we deserve to receive everything our heart desires that allows us to confidently know our miracles will happen. Each person has this ability and will use it when they are willing to make changes in their lives. Your willingness to do this in your life helps those around you do it in theirs.

It is our acknowledgement of our greatness that enables us to live lives that reflect that greatness.

It is our acknowledgement of our own power that enables us to live powerful lives.

It is our acknowledgement of our spiritual nature that allows us to fulfill our spiritual destiny as individuals and within the family of humanity.

And it is our acknowledgement of all of these things that will allow us to create miracles in our lives and for the world. For when each of us learns to live in the peace, joy, unconditional love, and gratitude that it takes to be in the miracle vibration, we will bring peace—and heaven—on earth.

When you began the 30 day miracle program were you feeling some doubt and uncertainty?

How has your life changed in the last 30 days and how much more confident are you in your ability to create miracles?

Do you feel more powerful, connected and confident of your power and spiritual connections? Creating miracles is our birthright and also the way we can live our lives, every day, using the universal energy to create the life of our dreams.

Acknowledging your ability to create miracles is your gift to yourself.

Using it in every area of your life to create effortless, joyful, abundant and miraculous living is your gift to the world and to humanity.

Final Thoughts

As we continue forward on our spiritual journey, for that is what life is, a spiritual journey that is fulfilled within the context of a human purpose, we learn new tools and information that make our journey easier. These tools help us move beyond our fears and old, limiting belief systems and learn to change our perspective about ourselves. To create a new reality we must first transform how we interpret what we perceive as our past 'failures', those things that didn't work out or that caused us pain or disappointment. One way to perceive them is to believe that we are imperfect, incapable and somehow unlucky, that nothing will work for us and that everything we try will not succeed.

The other is to recognize that our life is a journey of reconnection with our perfection and we created these life events to teach us to overcome, to learn from them how we disconnected from our power and figure out how to get reconnected to it. Each situation or lesson we learn from is another tool that we can use to move ahead on our spiritual path. The choice to stand still or move ahead is always up to us. Everything in our life is a choice and we always have the power to choose.

When you choose to live a miracle-filled life, you acknowledge your power and abilities. You also free yourself from the past and know that each moment is filled with potential and unlimited possibilities. Regrets, fear, and doubt cannot co-exist with miracle thinking. Your decision to manifest miracles in your life is one that includes leaving all past fear-based, limited thinking behind and allowing yourself the freedom to create the life that you choose, allowing peace, joy, unconditional love, and unlimited abundance, in whatever form that takes for you and whatever it means to you, to exist in your life.

This is a process that you can use every day of your life, to meet your every need. So have fun with it, be courageous in asking for exactly what you want and watch it appear in your life at exactly the right moment.

About Jennifer Hoffman

Jennifer Hoffman is a celebrated author, intuitive mystic, life and business evolution coach, international speaker, popular radio host, and creator of the celebrated Enlightening Life newsletter. Overcoming physical paralysis and surviving a near fatal car accident taught Jennifer how to transcend fear and master limitations, hallmarks of her teachings, to achieve total confidence and personal fulfillment. Since 2004 she has taught Miracle Coaching and published the weekly Enlightening Life newsletter, with more than 2 million weekly readers around the world, and has hosted the popular Enlightening Life radio show on Blog Talk Radio since 2008, to a weekly listening audience of millions.

Jennifer is internationally recognized for her work in the area of energy consciousness and empowerment, and thousands of students have completed and praise her Miracle Coaching, Raise your Vibes™ and High Vibes™ programs, offered through the High Vibes Living™ division of Enlightening Life OmniMedia. One of the world's top intuitives and spiritual teachers, her laser focused intuition allows her to identify and assess a client's past life traumas, present blocks, and future potential as she helps them master their learning, healing, growth, and transformation to create joy, passion, success, and abundance in life, love, career and business.

Jennifer's books include the acclaimed, top selling Ascending into Miracles and 30 Days to Everyday Miracles, as well as a number of digital books and programs. A masterful teacher and transformational speaker, Jennifer leads seminars and workshops around the world, virtually and in person.

Learn more about Jennifer's work at www.enlighteninglife.com

Jennifer Hoffman